# Garden
# lighting

# Garden
# lighting

**John Raine**

LAUREL
GLEN
San Diego, California

**Laurel Glen Publishing**
An imprint of the Advantage Publishers Group
5880 Oberlin Drive, San Diego, CA 92121-4794
www.advantagebooksonline.com

Copyright © 2001 Octopus Publishing Group Limited

ISBN 1-57145-692-9

Library of Congress Cataloging-in-Publication Data available upon
request.

Printed in China.

1  2  3  4  5    06  05  04  03  02

# contents

# Introduction

**above:** Illumination is provided by hidden light sources so the beauty of the garden scene is not compromised by the obvious presence of lighting hardware.

The basic function of lighting is to extend the hours in the day. Recent developments in lighting technology have encouraged us to look at how light sources are used as an integral part of the overall design, first in our homes and now in our gardens. The wider choice of products available lately, especially energy-saving and compact models, has made the addition of lighting to the garden both practical and affordable, and the increased use of lighting in public spaces has provided inspirational examples of how light can enhance or completely alter the appearance of buildings and structures. Increasingly, we see the garden as an extension of our indoor living space, and introducing lighting there will extend the time you can spend outdoors, give it a different appearance, and improve the security of your property.

## Outdoor rooms

Interest in both interior and garden design has increased during the last few years, and the desire to make the most of our personal space has been heightened by exposure to the makeover industry on television and in print. A garden provides valuable extra space, and using it as an outdoor room is an idea that has grown in popularity, even where it is sometimes too cool or wet for nighttime alfresco dining. Simply placing a table and chairs on a patio outside the French windows has developed into a more elaborate arrangement, and outdoor cooking, eating, entertainment, and relaxation now require a range of convenient services.

The outdoor room is now a concept central to garden design, and it is perhaps this more than anything else that has promoted a demand for stylish outdoor lighting. The barbecue area, patios, structures for shade and shelter, statuary, and planting can be enhanced by lighting that goes beyond the bright, functional output of a wall-mounted bulkhead light or floodlight. A garden that has been "designed"—that is, one that has focal points, structure in its layout, good planting, and a sense of perspective—is more likely

to benefit from lighting design. This need not mean a design undertaken by a professional garden designer or landscape architect—far from it, many amateur designs are inspired landscapes.

## Reversing the daylight effect

Daylight allows everything in the garden and its surroundings to be visible, because it is all lit by the sun. This is as true for a bare shed, neighboring houses, or power lines behind your prized statue, as it is for the pleasing features within the garden. When night falls, however, lighting can be used to

**above:** The uplighting of the small ornamental tree is framed by latticework columns which are illuminated by internally-mounted spotlights to create a more three-dimensional scene.

**below:** The ornamental lighting is complemented by terrace lighting, which can be controlled by a separate switch to cater for different uses of this "outdoor" room.

## Taking theater into the garden

Many techniques used in creative garden lighting derive from theater lighting, where they include creating atmosphere, molding a backdrop for the players, or even reinforcing the character of certain players, altering the perception of time and season, and changing the perspective itself so that the same set is viewed in contrasting ways for different scenes. Theater lighting is relatively powerful, and many of the tricks, such as subtly colored gels and beam control devices, like barn doors, are not easily weatherproofed at a smaller scale for exterior use. However, subtle theatrical effects can be achieved in the garden with miniaturized, low-power light sources that create focused beams of light.

## Practicality and creativity

A creative garden lighting scheme does not mean that you have to ignore or compromise the need for functional lighting. In homes and gardens, lighting is needed for safe access, security, and

**above:** Recessed uplights placed close to the base of the rocks emphasize the surface texture, as well as revealing color and shape against the dark backdrop of unlit trees.

**right:** An illuminated statue provides a beautiful focal point in a garden.

take control of what is seen. Apart from the effects of moonlight or glow from lights in the city, the rule is "if you don't light it, you won't see it." Dramatic directional lighting gives opportunities to create a fantasy scene by lighting water features and focal points, graceful trees, and architectural plants. Outdoor lighting can be more dramatic than interior illumination because most gardens are larger than any room. In addition to providing a visual panorama in the garden, lighting changes the way that an outdoor space is used. Entertaining on the patio or around the swimming pool, or just enjoying the expanse of the night sky overhead, become priorities when the weather warms up. Garden lighting will encourage alfresco activity by lighting paths and patios, and combining ornamental and functional lighting can change the feel of such areas to create a totally different experience.

such essential functions as transferring children and shopping bags from car to house. Alfresco dining is only the start of this story: task lighting to cook by, lighting to enable us to appreciate the appearance of food as well as its aroma and flavor, and amenity lighting to avoid tumbling down the steps from the kitchen are essential. In the dining room, the ceiling and walls provide lighting platforms for illuminating the table, the decor, and art. Outside, where there is no ceiling and there are probably fewer walls, substituting fresh air for interior decor demands alternative ways of creating interest in the surroundings, whether it be a panorama around the garden or the "furnishings" within—planting, focal points, decorative paving, or the sparkle of water. When the sun sets, creative garden lighting comes into its own.

## Creative garden lighting

Creative garden lighting concentrates on subtle schemes that create atmosphere and enhance the planting, garden features, and architecture,

**above:** Spotlighting the stone head provides a focal point among the general illumination of this alfresco dining area.

providing stimulating nighttime vistas. One thing to remember is that the choice of light fittings comes last. The aim is to create a beautifully illuminated garden where the light fittings are kept invisible as far as possible and where there is no glare from unshielded light sources at night. Who wants their visitors to exclaim at the light fittings rather than the plants, the graceful statue, or the serenity of the garden as a whole?

## The design approach

The creative use of light and shadow is the key to achieving good results, as only this will give depth and true interest in the view. Excessive lighting and the indiscriminate use of floodlights are common errors that result in garish illu-

**right:** Uplighting a statue against a dark background creates a focal point with stronger impact than it has in daylight.

**below:** Uplighting a mature tree adds vertical drama to the nighttime view of the illuminated garden.

mination and a "flat" perspective. "Painting with light" is the term often used to describe the techniques, although it is used in the artistic, selective sense rather than in the bland task of covering a wall. Creative garden lighting is concerned with illuminating features to exploit texture, form, and color in order to suggest a sense of depth. Combinations of light and shadow can create dramatic effects that are in complete contrast to the daylight scene.

Garden lighting can be all the more magical if the garden design has taken its use into account from the start in the choice of features, materials, and viewpoints. Just as good garden design will marry house to garden, so must the lighting. Downlighting on a terrace can be combined with subtle facade lighting to link the terrace and house, while the lighting for the front garden or drive should interpret the appearance of, and show the route through, the front of the property, as well as providing a welcoming focus for visitors when they arrive at the front door.

## Designing a lighting system

A creative lighting system is only partly a question of choosing the areas and features to light: it also involves a consideration of layout, function, and practicality. Selecting lighting subjects and techniques can never be divorced from the different uses of the garden, or parts of it, at night. For instance, a security light without a manual control switch would be inappropriate in an area with decorative lighting, and terrace wall lights are better if controlled by a different switch from the ornamental lighting circuit. Unless they have been chosen specifically to make a design statement—by an entrance, for example—light fittings need to be hidden or camouflaged wherever possible, so those that are recessed, small, or in a finish that blends in with the surroundings are desirable. Good lighting design depends fundamentally upon correct positioning and on selecting the correct lightbulb type, wattage, coverage, and beam angle.

This book aims to guide you through the whole design process, starting with explanations of some relevant lighting terminology and the types of light fittings available, progressing through the ways in which different types of lighting can be used around the garden, and an explanation of the lighting effects that can be achieved. The choice of lighting fittings and the methods for controlling lighting are described, and there is practical advice on how to implement designs. The emphasis throughout is on using lighting techniques with a professional standard of equipment and design to produce a truly impressive result. This book will appeal to homeowners who want to have a creative lighting design in their gardens and need an overview of the process. However, an expert should always be consulted before beginning a project, and proper safety precautions, local laws and guidelines, and manufacturers' instructions should always be followed.

**below:** A combination of lighting under the bridge, underwater lighting, and uplighting of the waterfalls brings this scene to life after dark.

# Lightbulbs and lighting

Visible light is the light that our eyes detect, and the aim of artificial lighting is, on the whole, to provide conditions that approximate natural light, so that we can see objects at night as we do during the day. To introduce a lighting system into your garden, you do not need to know that visible light is one of the types of radiation in the electromagnetic spectrum; nor do you need to know that the visible light spectrum ranges through the colors of the rainbow. It will be helpful, however, if you understand the properties of light that affect the ways in which artificial light can be used. If you appreciate how these properties can be used and exploited within your garden, lighting design can become truly creative.

### Light, lightbulbs, and fixtures

The terminology used to describe lights and lighting can be confusing. It has developed in a haphazard way and is defined differently in professional and in day-to-day usage. In addition, it varies from country to country. In this book the following terms are used.

•**Light** is a visual phenomenon; it is the beam or glow that is emitted by a bulb.

•**Lightbulb**, or lamp, is the source of light. The word can also apply to a tube, globe, reflector bulb, or capsule.

•**Fixture**, or luminaire, is the housing or body containing the holder or socket of a light source or bulb.

### Measures of light

Light levels in the garden at night contrast sharply with daylight levels: the brightest moonlight has only a fraction of the intensity of direct sunlight, but even at this level the human eye can perceive shape, color, and detail. It is generally the minimum level for path lighting domestic gardens. Against the background of such low ambient light levels in the garden at night, it is no surprise that even low levels of lighting achieve dramatic results.

The standard measure of output for bulbs is called a "lumen." The amount of illumination that a bulb provides is measured in foot candles. Bright moonlight is .09–.19 foot candles. In bulbs with reflectors, it is the intensity of the beam that matters, and that is measured in candelas.

### Brightness

In creative garden lighting, it is always important to avoid glare, which will instantly ruin an otherwise well-lit scene. Brightness and glare, however, are two sides of the same coin. A beam of light does not necessarily stop at the subject on which it is focused, and poorly positioned lighting or the wrong choice of light bulb or wattage can result in light straying in unwanted directions to produce glare. A common mistake is to place fixtures with overly bright bulbs near a front door in the belief that bright lighting is always good lighting. Although a high level of lighting is often intended to help the homeowner identify a visitor, lighting the person rather than the entrance and its approach is intimidating rather than welcoming, because it produces glare at eye level. The light itself becomes the focus of attention rather than the area or object that it is meant to illuminate.

### Glare

Glare is a common problem, especially if the light source itself is visible. There are two main types of glare:

•**Discomfort glare** is the name given to the type of light in which it is possible to perform a desired function but with some degree of discomfort. We have to squint through the glare toward an object or shield our eyes with a hand in order to see the illuminated area below or beyond the glare.

•**Disability glare** is the term for the light in which normal vision is impossible, and we may even become disoriented because nothing useful is visible. It is often the result of unexpected exposure to very bright lighting and is the theory behind security floodlighting.

**below:** Illumination of the garden scene should ensure that glare from the chosen fixtures is eliminated.

## Distance and angle of light

The amount of light we choose to shine from a light fitting toward an object is only the starting point, and other factors, including distance and the angle of the light, must also be considered. The apparent brightness of light falling on an object is affected by a number of factors. The farther away the lightbulb is from the subject, the brighter the light source must be to achieve the same effect. A further variable is the angle at which the light strikes a surface. If a circular beam is directed at right angles to a wall it will provide a circle of light of a given level. If the light strikes the same surface at the same distance from the same bulb but from a different angle, however, the same amount of light is spread over a larger, oval area. The light level is reduced by a factor relating to the angle at which the light strikes the surface. In addition, our perception of the brightness of light depends to some extent on what other lighting is around it: a single accent light will appear brighter if there is little ambient light than if there are other similar areas of light nearby. This is because the human eye adapts to light and dark by opening and closing the iris. This may all seem complicated, but in succeeding chapters we will see how flexibility in a lighting design will allow us to experiment with, and customize, the lighting effect.

## Reflectance

The word "reflectance" is used to describe the percentage of light reflected from a surface. Dark colors reflect much less light than lighter colors and also absorb more light than they reflect. Rough surfaces scatter light and significantly reduce the amount reflected toward the eye compared to smooth surfaces. The box on page 15 indicates the reflectance of various materials common in gardens and the practical implications when choosing which lightbulb power to use. The concept may seem academic, but the result is practical—for example, what brightness of lightbulb do you need to light a white marble statue in your garden and how is this light requirement affected if you replace it with a dark bronze subject?

## Choosing lightbulbs

Good lighting is fundamentally about choosing the right bulb for the job. The lightbulb or halogen bulb provides a light output appropriate for lighting a patio, illuminating the route from the car to the house, or providing lighting around the front door. Wall lights are typical uses for halogen lightbulbs. Tubular and compact fluorescent bulbs and many of the types used in street lighting come into this category; they provide an all-around light that diffuses in all directions unless controlled or directed by an external reflector. Garden lighting is principally about creating effects, and it requires a considerable degree of control in the direction of the light source. Creative garden lighting cannot generally be achieved by diffusion light sources; instead, we use reflector bulbs. These are bulbs that use a reflective coating or a shaped mirror surface to project a controlled beam of

**below:** Uplighting the apple tree complements the "moon lighting" of the path meandering alongside it. The overall impression is a mellow one, suited to the ambience of an out-of-town garden, and results from choosing low-voltage, wide-angle bulbs.

light. Only a few diffusion light sources are used in garden lighting, including metal halide bulbs, and their small size makes them suitable for use with external reflectors to produce controlled beams of light.

## Color rendering

We take the natural color of daylight for granted and assume that artificial lighting should strive to match it, a phenomenon known as "color rendering." Bulbs are rated on a scale out of 100, and the higher the number, the more natural the lit subject appears—80 out of 100, for instance means the light provides good color rendering. Color rendering is not always the most important factor in the choice of bulbs, however. Street lighting mainly uses sodium lighting, as its high energy-efficiency and long bulb life outweigh its awful orange-colored light output. Fortunately, most other light sources aim at a closer approximation to daylight. Metal halide sources and halogen bulbs provide particularly good color rendering.

**above:** White walls have a high reflectance; relatively low levels of light can be used to light the walls and throw the spiral topiary into silhouette.

| REFLECTANCE OF LANDSCAPE SURFACES | | |
|---|---|---|
| **MATERIAL** | **REFLECTANCE (%)** | **LIGHTING LEVEL REQUIRED TO ACHIEVE EQUAL BRIGHTNESS (FOOT CANDLES)** |
| White paint | 75 | 12.36 |
| Light stone or brick | 50 | 18.58 |
| White marble | 45 | 20.90 |
| Concrete | 40 | 23.23 |
| Red brick | 30 | 32.52 |
| Vegetation | 25 | 37.16 |
| Slate | 18 | 51.10 |
| Dark stone | 18 | 51.10 |
| Asphalt | 7 | 130.06 |
| Moist soil | 7 | 130.06 |
| Grass | 6 | 154.77 |

## Color temperature

Another measure for lightbulb types provides a relative indication of the color of light. This is the color temperature, which is expressed in degrees Kelvin or K (273K is equal to 32° F). What might be thought of as warm colors—yellows and oranges—are, in fact, at a lower temperature than the cool blues (see table below). Halogen and the 3000K metal halide bulbs are among the most pleasing to use in garden-lighting design because their fairly white light tends to flatter the natural colors of flowers, foliage, and building materials, and fits in with our perception of "natural" color. Fluorescent bulbs are available in a range from warm to cool white for different applications. Warm white is favored in most gardens because it resembles the color of halogen lighting, which has a mellow look. Cool white, on the other hand, tends to look harsh.

## Lightbulb life

Lightbulb life is another factor to consider, particularly for lighting that is in regular use—for example, if it is switched on every night by a timer or photocell. Bulb life is rated in units of 1000 hours and is given by manufacturers as an average bulb life (see table on page 17). Think of 1000 hours as being the equivalent of switching on your garden lighting for three hours every night of the year: a bulb with a life of 1000 hours will, therefore, last roughly a year. Halogen bulbs produce light by incandescence— that is, passing electricity through a filament to heat it until it glows. Other types of "discharge" bulbs produce light by using electricity to strike an arc through a gas-filled tube or envelope in such a way that either the gas or a coating on the inside of the envelope "fluoresces" or glows. These bulbs also use less energy and are becoming increasingly popular for wall lights and lantern fittings. Long-life, high-intensity discharge bulbs, such as the metal halide types, are used for uplighting large trees.

## Energy efficiency

Energy efficiency is another advantage of halogen bulbs. Not only do halogen capsule and reflector bulbs run on 12

| LIGHTBULB | COLOR TEMPERATURE (K) | COLOR/TONE |
|---|---|---|
| Sodium street lighting | 1800–2000 | Orange/warm |
| Halogen | 2900–3000 | White |
| Metal halide | 3000–6000 | White or blue/cool |
| Mercury vapor | 3500–4000 | Blue/cool |

volts—a safer voltage to have outdoors—but they are also very efficient. Use of halogen gas inside the glass capsule around the filament recycles halogen shed by the filament and enables the bulb to operate at a higher temperature and for longer. This doubles both the bulb life and the light output per watt compared to a typical halogen bulb. Compact fluorescent bulbs typically use about 20 percent of the power of a halogen bulb for the same light output. For higher power applications, such as uplighting large trees, a metal halide bulb will typically save more than 85 percent of the energy of a halogen bulb or 75 percent of the energy of a linear halogen floodlight bulb doing the same job.

## Choosing a system

Depending on your requirements, each type of commonly used lighting system has its advantages and disadvantages in terms of cost, color, energy efficiency, and flexibility.

### Halogen projector bulbs

The mainstay of garden lighting for many years was the PAR type of bulb. PAR stands for Parabolic Aluminized Reflector, and the most common example is the PAR38 bulb, a reflector bulb, 4$^3/_4$ inches in diameter, usually with an Edison screw base or cap, and intended for use in a line-voltage spike- or wall-mounted holder. This type of bulb has always been relatively inexpensive and widely available, and requires little specialized knowledge to use to create a simple lighting scheme. One drawback is that it is mainly available in higher wattages, from 60 watts upward, but it is a popular bulb for the general uplighting of trees. In this role, a spot or flood beam is suitable for lighting columnar and spreading trees. It is available with color coatings, usually green, red, yellow, and blue, but this kind of color treatment of natural subjects in a garden often produces a garish effect, which overwhelms rather than reinforces the natural appearance of

| BULB | TYPICAL LIFE (hours) |
|------|----------------------|
| Halogen | 1000 |
| Halogen capsule | 2000 |
| Halogen spotlight | 3000–4000 |
| Compact fluorescent | 5000–10,000 |
| Metal halide | up to 10,000 |

foliage, stone, and timber. A green bulb tends to make a specimen tree or shrub look like a plastic Christmas tree.

### Halogen dichroic bulbs

Creative garden lighting has recently come to be dominated by the MR16 low-voltage halogen bulb. This 2-inch diameter bulb features a miniature halogen capsule

**above:** The bluish hue of the tree is a result of uplighting with a mercury vapor bulb; this contrasts with the color achieved by illuminating the statues with white light from halogen bulbs.

| COMPARISONS OF LIGHTBULBS WITHOUT REFLECTORS OR FOR USE WITH EXTERNAL REFLECTORS | | | | | |
|---|---|---|---|---|---|
| BULB SHAPE | BULB TYPE | BULB LIFE (hours) | EFFICIENCY (Lumens per watt) | COLOR TEMPERATURE (K) | FEATURES AND APPLICATIONS IN EXTERIOR LIGHTING |
| | halogen bulb | 1000 | 9–13 | 2700 | **Pros:** Low-cost, familiar product provides warm lighting in wall lights **Cons:** Poor energy efficiency and bulb life |
| | halogen capsule | 2000 | 15–25 | 2900 | **Pros:** Twice the bulb life and energy efficiency of a halogen bulb, white light, miniature size **Cons:** 12 volt—needs transformer |
| | halogen linear | 2000 | 15–20 | 3000 | **Pros:** High-power, white light for floodlighting **Cons:** High power consumption; unsuitable for focused lighting |
| | compact fluorescent | 5000–10000 | 50–65 | 2900–4000 | **Pros:** Long bulb life, good energy efficiency, warm and cool colors **Cons:** Coiled tubes not attractive but new bulb shapes appearing |
| | metal halide (ceramic) | 9000 | 80–100 | 3000–4200 | **Pros:** High energy efficiency, long life, choice of white and cool light good for focused lighting of trees, etc. **Cons:** Fixtures fairly expensive |
| | mercury vapor | 12000–24000 | 19–63 | 3500–4000 | **Pros:** Good energy efficiency and life **Cons:** Fixtures relatively expensive, cool bluish light not suitable for many applications |
| | high pressure sodium | 14000–55000 | 66–140 | 2000 | **Pros:** Exceptional bulb life and high energy efficiency, popular for street and commercial lighting **Cons:** Orange color rendering |
| | low pressure sodium | 16000 | 100–198 | 1800 | **Pros:** Exceptional energy efficiency and long life popular for street lighting **Cons:** Orange color rendering |

bulb mounted in a multimirror reflector to provide a controlled beam of light with little peripheral light spill. These bulbs run on 12 volts, so, although transformers must be installed, they permit flexible cabling configurations and easy adjustment.

The MR16 is twice as energy efficient as the PAR38 halogen bulb. The "dichroic" reflector reflects all the light forward, while allowing much of the heat to dissipate through the rear of the bulb—that is, it projects much less heat toward your planting or down onto the dining table. MR16 bulbs are available in wattages from 10 to 75 and beam angles from 7 to 60 degrees, giving much more choice in accurately and precisely lighting subjects without glare. The wide range of bulb choices is reinforced by its small size: it is less than half the diameter of a PAR38 bulb and about 10 percent of its overall size. Using MR16 bulbs means that fixtures can be much smaller and yet produce more light than old-fashioned halogen fittings, allowing much greater flexibility in their use.

## Positioning

When you are choosing subjects to light in a garden, it does not necessarily follow that a higher wattage bulb will produce a brighter effect. Spotlighting by using a narrow-beam halogen bulb will produce a more intense circle of light than a wider beam of the same wattage, and a narrow-beam reflector more tightly focuses the light emitted by the halogen capsule into a higher concentration in a smaller circle. This not only makes best use of the wattage capability of a lightbulb but also serves to make the subject that is being lit more prominent than the other objects around it. A narrow-beam, 20-watt bulb can provide a much higher light level in the center of its beam than a wide-angle, 50-watt bulb in which the light is not focused so tightly. Perhaps surprisingly, therefore, higher-wattage, wide-beam bulbs are often used for the general illumination of mature shrub borders and spreading trees, while lower-wattage, narrower-beam bulbs are used to accent individual features. The table below summarizes and compares the characteristics of halogen PAR38 and halogen reflector bulbs and details the advantages and disadvantages of using each. There is also an indication of the ways in which each lightbulb can be used in the garden.

**above:** An MR16 halogen reflector bulb is about one-tenth of the overall size of a PAR38 halogen projector bulb, but provides the same light output.

| COMPARISONS OF REFLECTOR BULBS | | | | | |
|---|---|---|---|---|---|
| **BULB SHAPE** | **BULB TYPE** | **BULB LIFE (hours)** | **EFFICIENCY (Candelas per watt)** | **COLOR TEMPERATURE (K)** | **FEATURES AND APPLICATIONS IN EXTERIOR LIGHTING** |
| | halogen PAR38 projector (flood 30° beam) | 1000–2000 | 20–24 | 2700 | **Pros:** Low-cost, familiar product provides warm lighting<br>**Cons:** Poor energy efficiency and bulb life; limited range of beam angles and wattages; large size |
| | halogen reflector (flood 36° beam) | 3000–5000 | 50 | 3000 | **Pros:** White light, small size, twice bulb life and energy efficiency of halogen projector bulb, wide choice of beam angles and wattages (10–75 watts)<br>**Cons:** 12 volts—needs transformer |

# Types of garden lighting

**above:** Bollard lights illuminate this steep flight of steps to provide safe access; line-voltage bollard lights provide high light output that is often more functional than decorative.

Designing a garden lighting scheme is not just a question of selecting from among the range of wall-mounted, recessed, or spike-mounted lights. It is also important to distinguish the ways in which power can be introduced into the garden and to match the different types of light sources that are available to the appropriate features. Steps, for example, will be lit in a quite different way from a specimen tree, or the area around a barbecue.

## Types of light fittings

One of the problems with introducing lighting into the garden is that the names given to light fittings are either confusing or apparently inappropriate or both. Some names simply express what a light fitting does—floodlights and spotlights, for example. Other names, however, may describe the ways in which the fitting is mounted (wall lights and step lights), its direction (uplights and downlights), its power source (solar lights and low-voltage lights) or its function (security lights). Other names have a historical, rather than a functional, resonance—the term "bulkhead lights" derives from the original maritime usage, "coach lamps" dates from the days of horse power, and "lanterns" remind us of the time when this was a convenient way of carrying a candle or oil lamp.

## Line-voltage lighting

Until a couple of decades ago, nearly all lighting was line voltage—that is, it was powered from the household current, usually somewhere between 110 and 120 volts. The light sources that were used in garden lighting were predominantly the halogen lightbulb for wall lights, lanterns of various types, and PAR projector bulbs, mainly the PAR38 bulb, rated at 60–120 watts. These sources still survive in residential use, partly because of their low initial cost and partly because energy-saving lighting and lighting design in the home are far from widely employed or understood among nonspecialists.

Of the more modern line-voltage light sources, compact fluorescent bulbs are gradually taking over from halogen in exterior wall lights and lanterns, while metal halide high-pressure discharge lighting is becoming the main way of uplighting large trees and architectural features. Metal halide floodlights and uplights provide a range of energy-efficient lighting power beyond that which can be handled by 12-volt equipment.

## Low-voltage lighting

In low-voltage systems, line voltage is reduced through a transformer to 12 or 24 volts, which is a safer level of voltage. This means that flexible wires can be used around the garden rather than the fixed wiring required for line-voltage systems.

The use of low-voltage lighting in gardens originates from two sources. First, low-voltage halogen lighting was originally developed for lighting store displays and works of art in museums and art galleries. This was recognized as the means by which theater lighting techniques could be miniaturized and transferred to landscape lighting. This was adopted mainly for commercial and public applications initially, but it is now increasingly used for private gardens. Second, automotive halogen bulbs were adopted as a simple means

**below:** A low-voltage spreadlight provides a pool of light around a path or low planting, while hiding the light source under the "hat" on top.

of providing low-power illumination in the garden from a transformer in the house, avoiding the need to lay protected line-voltage wiring outside.

### Garden-lighting kits

The market for garden-lighting kits developed rapidly as fittings made from inexpensive materials, especially plastic, made garden lighting more affordable. Some manufacturers built transformers into weatherproof boxes and adopted thicker low-voltage wiring so that lighting could be extended further out into the garden, and used metal fittings that could withstand the heat of a higher-power bulb. More recently, the original halogen bulbs have been increasingly replaced by more efficient, longer-life, halogen reflector bulbs in spotlights and halogen capsule bulbs in step and path lights.

Commercial landscape lighting aside, the garden-lighting market has tended to polarize into "professional" garden lighting, principally distributed by lighting or landscape specialists offering related design services, and the retail sector, offering a combination of inexpensive halogen PAR38 line-voltage lighting and plastic low-voltage garden-lighting kits.

Most garden retail outlets offer at least one kind of garden-lighting kit. It will usually include light fittings made from plastic to reduce cost and for easy assembly, and require few tools and little electrical knowledge. The lights are attached to a ribbed wire by clamp-on connectors, in which sharp contacts pierce the insulation to make contact with the conducting wires inside. The low-voltage wire connects easily to a transformer, which is usually designed

---

### LOW-VOLTAGE LIGHTING

Where lights are to be used near the house, the transformer can be located inside the house and either plugged or cabled into a socket or other electrical outlet, which is operated by a switch or simple cableless timer. The low-voltage cable can be taken outside through a hole drilled in the wall and the fixtures connected to it. The cable should be protected in a conduit under paving or through gravel or hard-core layers, but can otherwise be run on the surface of the soil, hidden by low planting or a layer of mulch.

Low-power plastic fixtures may clip on to the cable, whereas higher-power metal fixtures will usually require a cable joint using screw-nuts, crimp connectors, or terminal blocks. Transformers meant for "interior use only" should never be used outside. Low-power, low-voltage lights may be sited only up to 60 feet from the transformer. For lights further from the house or of 20 watts or more in power, install exterior transformers and line-voltage exterior cabling to the transformer locations.

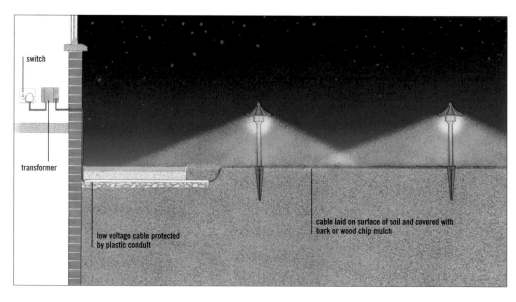

switch

transformer

low voltage cable protected by plastic conduit

cable laid on surface of soil and covered with bark or wood chip mulch

**left:** A typical low-cost, low-voltage kit for path lighting, consisting of a transformer for interior installation, cable, and plastic fixtures with low-voltage bulbs.

**below:** This plastic bollard light is from a low-voltage kit powered from an interior transformer. It illuminates a small area of paving or low planting. As the bulb is low power, glare from the unshielded light source is unlikely to be a problem.

for interior use.

The limiting factor is the material from which the lights are made, which is usually solid copper or molded plastic. Most plastics deform in close proximity to heat, so the bulbs used tend to be relatively low power, often 10 watts or below. Although some are available as spotlights, the majority are designed as miniature lanterns, globes, or as a "pagoda" design, and their main role tends to be marking out a path or perhaps providing low-level lighting by steps or a patio. The low power limits their usefulness in larger gardens or for lighting anything but smaller garden features. They are, however, a means of providing safe lighting where the installation of line-voltage cables along walls or structures, or in trenches at a safe depth would be impossible or, at least, too disruptive to be practical.

Kits are also often a useful way to experiment, which may later lead a homeowner to consider a scheme using higher-power metal products for larger features or areas in the garden.

It is important to check whether the transformer is suitable for use indoors, in the house, garage, or an outbuilding only. If a transformer suitable for exterior use is provided and that is where you wish to locate it, you should budget for the services of a professional electrician to install it.

### Solar lighting

The idea behind self-contained, solar-

powered lighting products is the same as for garden-lighting kits: the provision of low-power garden lighting without the need for line-voltage cabling. Common forms include miniature lanterns or pagodas. A small photovoltaic solar panel on top of each fixture charges an internal battery by day, and the light is switched on by a photocell at dusk. Some models include a movement detector to switch on the light when someone passes by. The light sources are usually fairly low power to strike a balance between brightness and battery life. How long they remain lit obviously depends on the power of the light source, the size of the battery, and the extent of recharge provided by the duration and intensity of sunlight. Brighter models may boast five hours of lighting after recharge in bright sunlight, whereas other models are lower powered and are intended mainly for marking a path. Solar lights can be rather inconsistent and some makes are unattractive.

The battery will need to be replaced at regular intervals. Nickel cadmium batteries usually need to be replaced after about 500 cycles, which is about

**below:** This small solar light is designed to mark the route along the edge of a path rather than light a particular area. The compact design features a small solar-electric cell which provides limited recharge capacity for a battery and a low-wattage bulb.

18 months of daily use. A more professional standard of lighting and electrical power can be achieved using a system of batteries charged from solar panels on a roof, but this type of specialty installation is outside the scope of this book.

### Directional lighting

Landscape lighting professionals use projector types of bulb, particularly low-voltage halogen dichroic bulbs, but also other types of halogen bulbs and some high-pressure discharge types, such as metal halide bulbs, to create directional lighting. The range of bulb beams will range from "very narrow spot" to "very wide flood." It can be a spike-mounted spotlight, which performs the function of uplighting, or wall-mounted, which performs the function of downlighting. The terms "uplight," "uplighter," "downlight," and "downlighter" also

**left.** Regularly spaced spread lights provide effective path lighting without detracting from other illuminated garden features along the route.

describe products that perform those lighting functions.

## Path and step lights

Paths and steps are often lit with spotlights mounted on structures or trees. Where there are no such lighting positions, specific lights need to be incorporated in the lighting design to fulfill this function. Where there are flanking walls, the use of discreet, surface, recessed step or brick lights provides localized lighting. In the absence of walls, the choice is often between spread lights (lights on a stick) and bollard lights (lights in a stick). These products may also be used to provide low-level lighting around patios and drives, while area lighting products (see below) may also be used if higher light levels are required.

**left:** Spike-mounted halogen spotlights are versatile tools for lighting a range of subjects. This type of copper spotlight weathers to an attractive mottled brown finish and can utilize a variety of bulb wattages and beam angles to produce different effects.

**above:** Area lighting of steps is effective for access purposes, but produces a bland effect devoid of features or emphasis.

### Area lighting

Providing lighting across a horizontal area is usually the preserve of line-voltage lighting, largely because a wide choice of fixtures is available in finishes to suit all architectural styles. Although the mounting position may vary from wall mount or pillar top, to column or pole mount, such lights rely mainly on "diffusion" light sources to spread light around them, although some models have internal reflectors to maximize the outward spread of light.

### Floodlights

Floodlighting aims to reproduce the all-embracing illumination of the sun. It is seen at its most extreme form in sports stadiums, where the aim is to allow sports to be conducted in conditions as near to daylight as possible. This is not what garden lighting is about. There are some requirements for high levels of lighting in gardens for which floodlighting may be appropriate—a tennis court, perhaps, or an area where horses are kept in the country. In suburban gardens, the need is usually more for lighting the children's football game on the lawn or downlighting paved areas for parties.

### Security lights

Floodlighting is often thought of as the only means of security lighting, but there are alternatives (see pages 38–39). The term "security light" is usually associated with an individual floodlight or wall-mounted fixture with a built-in movement detector that switches on the light when an intruder comes within the zone of coverage. The use of built-in detectors is often a cost consideration rather than one aimed at providing optimum performance: such fixtures are often less expensive but easier to fit on a do-it-yourself basis.

### Linear lighting

Lighting a structure or a linear feature has, until recently, been largely achieved by projecting a beam of light toward it or by placing fixtures to diffuse light onto it. In recent years, trends in lighting technology have conspired to produce a more novel approach called "outlining," either using the light sources themselves to emphasize the linearity or using a hidden array of light to provide a linear effect. Each type of product tends to have its own associated lighting effect, so these are dealt with here, rather than in later chapters. Some types of lighting, such as cold cathode and neon lighting, are used by professionals; they require customized configuration and would be too complex to install in most gardens. The principal products used in garden lighting are string lighting, tape lighting, and fiber-optic lighting.

## String lighting

String lighting is most familiar as the small lights strung on Christmas trees, as the bulb life is quite short. Most Christmas lighting products are 110 volts and are described as being suitable for exterior use, however, be sure to read the instructions and safety information on the package carefully. Employ a professional electrician for more elaborate string-lighting schemes that you wish to enjoy year-round.

A variation on this theme is rope lighting where a lighting string is threaded through a clear, flexible, plastic hose. The bulb life is also relatively short, but this is a popular form of inexpensive outdoor lighting for parties and other festive occasions. Christmas-tree lighting is usually a zigzag effect of lighting strung around the tree, while rope lighting is often wound around the trunks of palm trees

in Middle Eastern countries. Rope light is usually a 110-volt product, so proper installation outside is essential, and use near water is not advised. All exterior 110 volt AC outlets by code in the U.S. must be protected by a Ground Fault Interrupter (GFI).

### Long-life string lighting

If you have a bigger budget you may consider a more permanent display. Commercial string lighting uses Xenon bulbs, which last up to 20,000 hours. This means that you can put the string lights up in a tree and just switch them on when you want to instead of putting temporary ones up every time Christmas or a party comes around.

The most stylish way of using string lighting in anything other than a dense

**above:** Lighting emphasizes hard landscaping, which can produce an effect described as "stark" or "minimalist," depending on your point of view.

**left:** Ornamental lanterns can be chosen for decorative purposes, as well as for garden illumination.

conifer is to achieve an outlining effect on a tree with a less-dense canopy. Fix the string lighting up the trunk and along the branches so that the finished effect is of lines of lights tracing out the structure of the tree. Tie the string into place with biodegradable garden twine, which will break if the tree outgrows its grip; do not use plastic fixings, such as plastic electrical ties or metal wire, because they could strangle a growing branch. If wire clips need to be fixed to the trunk, use stainless-steel pins; never use brass screws, as they poison many types of trees. The bulbs are typically under $1/2$ inch in diameter and are rated at around 1 watt each. Commercial Christmas tree lighting for public displays often uses higher-power lighting in globes, but only professional electricians should install these.

## Tape lighting

Outlining is not used only for trees. In many countries it is used widely as a means of lighting a gazebo or pergola, partly to outline the structure and partly to provide some subtle lighting for the area within. Some people regard this type of lighting as too much like that found in a theme park or pleasure beach for a domestic lighting role model, but in a modern garden used as an outdoor room such lighting can provide excitement all year round.

Outlining has further developed to provide linear lighting in a more easily concealed strip format. The conductors are contained within a flat, insulated plastic tape, which can be fixed to flat surfaces, or in miniature versions where the light string is concealed within plastic or metal strip for fixing under steps, for example. Light-emitting diodes with a long bulb life are currently being tipped

**right:** Linear lighting outlines the structure of the gazebo and provides some ambient lighting within.

as a successor for existing exterior light sources. They may feature in further developments of tape light, but at present they have not achieved widespread commercial use.

### Fiber-optic lighting

Fiber-optic lighting is often described as a new technology, but it has been around for more than 20 years. It is available in two forms: side-emitting and end-emitting. Side-emitting fiber is used for outlining. Optical glass fibers are bundled together in a clear sleeve, so the light is projected along the entire wire from a remotely mounted control box containing a focused bulb assembly designed for the purpose. In end-emitting fiber-optic lighting, the glass fibers are encased in a black sheath, and the light is emitted at the end of each "tail" running from the control box. It is focused through a glass lens to provide a pinpoint of light or to project a beam of light on a subject.

While fiber-optic lighting is still relatively expensive for widespread use in domestic gardens, its appeal lies in the fact that the fiber-optic cable carries no heat or electricity, which makes it

very useful in water features. Only one bulb needs to be replaced for a whole lighting array, and a color-wheel option means that changing color effects can be achieved fairly simply, if required. Popular applications include outlining around the edge of a pool and accent lighting within complex water features, where electric lighting would be difficult to install or where it would be difficult to change bulbs. However, fiber-optic lighting is not a general-purpose product, and each installation needs to be precisely engineered. Ducting into the features in which it is installed can be equally complex, so it is essential to get help from a professional.

**above:** String lighting adds an unusual touch to this line of espalier apple trees in winter.

# The purpose
# of lighting

**above:** Underwater lighting of the wall fountain is framed by the lighting of the large urns, drawing the eye downward in this courtyard and away from the city lights outside. Downlighting the paved area adds foreground illumination for alfresco dining.

When you start to think about designing a lighting system for your garden you must first understand the roles lighting will play in the use and enjoyment of each part of your exterior space. The way you will use the garden and your choice of lighting will have fundamental implications for the planning of the system, including the sources of power, the number of circuits, and the position and type of controls.

## Choosing a type of lighting

Begin by dividing the garden into areas that you know will be used differently, and draw up a table to facilitate detailed planning later. Then, within each area, look at your lighting needs.

### Identifying your lighting needs

Before you can draw up a plan of a lighting scheme, decide what you will use the lighting for. There are five main types of lighting:

- **Ornamental lighting** is used when garden features are lit for visual appeal.
- **Amenity lighting** is introduced for safety and practical purposes—for example, on a patio to light a dining area, on a driveway, or near steps to make them safer.
- **Task lighting** makes it possible to carry out specific jobs, such as cooking on a barbecue or getting objects from an outbuilding.
- **Access lighting** permits safe movement around the garden by lighting paths, steps, doors, and water.
- **Security lighting** deters intruders, creates an illusion of occupation, and reassures home-owners.

There may be some overlap. You may write "ornamental/access" for an area in which ornamental lighting to enhance an area must be complemented by safe path illumination—for example, in a woodland walk. In the same way, "access/ornamental" would be appropriate for where good path lighting is required between the house and a swimming pool, but where there are also trees and shrubs that should be lit to provide interest along the way. Some specific types of lighting may apply to certain areas—floodlighting for the tennis court and underwater lighting in the swimming pool, for example, but, at this stage, concentrate on summarizing as simply as possible what you believe each area requires and the order of priority between the functions. Your table will develop further as you choose the lighting effects and start the detailed planning of the installation.

## Ornamental lighting

A good start in developing a garden lighting plan is to focus first on the ornamental lighting effects you want to achieve and the areas of the garden in which they will be applied, as we usually expect that lighting in all or most areas will have at least some ornamental value. Ask yourself the following questions:

- Do I want to see this lighting only when I am in the garden?
- Do I want to see this lighting only when I am in the house and, if so, from which rooms?
- Do I want to see this lighting from both inside and outside, and, if so, from which rooms or areas?
- Will I see this lighting only from a selected viewpoint inside the house or outside the house?
- Should the ornamental lighting primarily provide a welcoming view of the house?

This may all seem obvious, but some homeowners see lighting only as a means of prolonging their enjoyment of warm evenings in the garden, while those who live in less temperate areas will need the illuminated view from the

**below:** Uplighting from below galvanized mesh reflects from mirrors and galvanized planters to provide a subtle setting for architectural planting.

| Area of garden | Type of lighting |
|---|---|
| **Ornamental garden areas** (water features, trees, etc.) | Ornamental lighting |
| **Driveways** | Amenity and security lighting |
| **Paths and steps** | Access and ornamental lighting |
| **Entrances** | Access, ornamental, and security lighting |
| **Sitting and eating areas** | Amenity and task lighting |
| **Activity areas** (swimming pools, tennis courts, etc.) | Access lighting and other lighting specific to the function |

**below:** Lighting a view out of the window is the main requirement when cooler or wetter evenings are more common.

house. Do not make the mistake of thinking that ornamental lighting is only about creating dramatic focal points. Drama can be created when and where you want, but the aim of ornamental lighting is usually to create an atmosphere and a balanced view of the garden that is easy on the eye.

**Identifying viewpoints**
The next requirement is to establish the viewpoints from which these areas of the garden and the features within them may be seen. This will determine the complexity of your lighting system. In a

small garden the answer may be a simple one. If the reception rooms face the rear garden so that all or most of it can be seen from all of the rear windows, for example, and the patio is immediately adjacent to the house, a simple, single-circuit, ornamental lighting system is likely to be adequate. All the ornamental lighting will be switched on together, and all the lighting will be appreciated from any viewpoint on the patio or in the house.

You are, however, also likely to have some lights on the wall of the house to provide lighting for other purposes, such

as lighting the patio area for dining, barbecuing, or perhaps for safe passage to a side gate, shed, or garage. If such cabling is possible, it will be useful to have separate switches for the wall lights and the garden lighting on the same switch panel, conveniently located by one or more of the doors or windows facing the rear garden.

In larger gardens or in properties with a more complex building or garden layout, more thought will be needed. Establishing viewpoints for individual areas or features from different rooms or outside seating areas will help to determine the lighting design and how the system should be cabled and controlled. If different areas of the garden are visible only from certain viewpoints, there may be little point in switching on all the lighting in the whole garden if only one area can be seen

from the room most commonly in use. Even if you wish to have a central switch panel for all the lighting—in a central hallway, for example—you may still wish to control the lighting in separate areas in different ways.

## Amenity lighting

Once you have developed your ideas for ornamental lighting, you should think about potential requirements in other areas, such as providing lighting for practical activities and ensuring that the lighting also means a safe garden and a secure home. General lighting that enables you to perform a range of functions, from inserting a key in a lock to seeing the meal you are about to enjoy, to avoiding stepping on children's toys that have been left on the terrace, is known as amenity lighting. Normally, this requirement is

**above:** Ornamental lighting of statues, trees, and shrubs provides a continuous vista around the pool, while underwater lighting diffuses to provide general illumination of the poolside.

**above:** Uplighting reflects from the white walls to provide illumination within a small courtyard garden, helping to distract the eye from the surrounding buildings.

perhaps halogen capsule bulbs for small areas. These will usually be fixed on the face of the building, mounted on top of a garden wall or gate pillar, or supported on a post or column of one size or another. They diffuse lighting all around and downward, and many designs will be partially shielded to avoid projecting light upward to pollute the night sky or to annoy your neighbors.

The style chosen should reflect the architectural character of your house and your own taste. A general-purpose bulb holder (a bayonet cap or Edison screw, for example) gives flexibility in the choice of bulb type and wattage. These choices are often a compromise between the maximum heat permissible within the fixture, the light output required, the appearance of the bulb, and the color of the light emitted.

Floodlighting is rarely satisfactory for amenity lighting in private gardens, unless it is on a separate circuit that can be switched on only when higher-power lighting is required, such as retrieving objects from an area or providing adequate lighting when there are a lot of people at a function. Even then, the power should be limited to 150 watts per floodlight because above this level glare starts to become a significant problem. Higher-power floodlighting should be reserved for sporting activities and security lighting, and even then it should be installed to be effective only within the property boundary.

fulfilled by area lighting, although occasionally fixtures placed for decorative effect also fulfill the role of amenity lighting. Recessed downlights under a porch canopy, for example, perform the decorative function of illuminating a front door and creating a welcome focal point for anyone approaching the house, but they also provide enough light to light your way through the door and safely over the step. Downlighting from a pergola or from under the eaves of a house are ways of using directional lighting for a patio.

## Area lighting

Where there is no convenient structure for an overhead lighting platform, most amenity lighting is provided by general area lighting—fixtures with halogen bulbs, compact fluorescent bulbs, or

## Task lighting

Daylight is normally associated with carrying out tasks outside, whether it be gardening or chopping logs, but there are tasks performed during leisure time for which lighting is essential, like carrying dishes from the kitchen to the patio table. While you are introducing cables to your garden and home to provide ornamental and amenity lighting, make sure you give yourself flexibility and choice so that you can use the lighting to its fullest extent.

If you include a separate,

left: Uplighting of the house facade, coupled with downlighting of the decking and linear lighting of the steps produces an impression that is both ornamental and practical.

weatherproof switch for task lighting around or above the barbecue, you will be able to switch it off when the cooking is finished so that you are not viewing the smoking remains while you dine. Equally, you probably do not want the door of the shed lit all evening for the sake of putting things away at the end of the evening. Defining these tasks at an early part of the planning stage means you can put convenient switches in the right places, probably at little extra cost.

## Access lighting

Access lighting is concerned mainly with lighting routes into and around the garden and house. The boundary between access and amenity lighting gets blurred the closer we get to the house or outbuildings, where lighting is associated with fetching and carrying, as opposed to just walking.

Access lighting can be achieved by a variety of techniques. Its purpose is primarily safety, yet it can also be seen partly as amenity lighting and partly as ornamental lighting. The primary need is

below: Uplighting and spreadlighting at intervals along this 400-foot driveway lined with *Cupressus leylandii* conspire to provide ornamental access lighting.

| SAFETY CHECKLIST | |
| --- | --- |
| **POTENTIAL DANGER** | **POSITION OF HAZARD** |
| Change of level | Steps, ramps, unfenced decks, or patios |
| Change of direction | Intersections or bends in paths |
| Entrances | Doors, gateways |
| Pedestrian routes | Driveways, paths |
| Paths near or over water | Bridges, stepping-stones, pool edges, or banks |
| Open areas used to travel around the garden | Terraces, patios, lawns, paved or graveled areas |
| Obstacles | Trees near paths, overhanging beams, or branches |
| Specific dangers | Barbecues, play equipment, moving machinery |

to ensure that the route is safe. It can be used to highlight areas that you need to see—the gate tucked into a hedge will not announce itself unless you have bothered to signal its presence with lighting. Access lighting should be used to light the driveway to the front door and also to highlight the door number and name. The approach should be well lit so that the visitor has a welcoming focus for direction.

Finally, don't treat the lighting of paths and driveways purely as a utilitarian exercise; consider ways to light planting and garden features along the way so that they act as attractive signposts to guide the visitor safely. For example, make the lighting entertaining by "moon lighting" down from trees to provide natural lighting for a driveway. The illusion of moonlight filtering down through branches and leaves to create dappled patterns of light and shadow on the area below is more aesthetically pleasing than installing bollard lights or "street" lights along the verge.

### Lighting for safety

Nowhere is good lighting practice more important than in lighting for access and safety. Making someone feel wholly disoriented when they reach the top of a flight of stairs by confronting them with the beam of a badly placed spotlight is as dangerous as failing to light the steps at all. Lighting for safety

**right:** The underwater lighting in the pool defines the area of hazard for anyone walking around this area of the garden.

can be achieved by a variety of techniques. For example, path lighting can be achieved by lighting provided for ornamental value (moon lighting from a tree), by specific access lighting (spread lights in adjacent planting), by area lighting on the walls of the house, or as the result of a task lighting requirement—getting barbecue lighting fluid from the shed, for example.

### A safety audit

Not all of the safety concerns listed above will arise in every garden, as garden designs are so individual and the way people use their garden at night varies widely. In a garden with no routes to the end of the garden for access to rear gates or sheds, it will not be necessary to light the lawn as if it were a path, but it would be possible to illuminate it as a "horizontal feature."

It is worth considering the safety aspects from two viewpoints: that of the homeowner who knows the layout and possible hazards in the garden, and that of a visitor who is unaware of any danger lurking in the dark. For the homeowner, good area lighting should have eliminated places where you might trip on an

**above:** Recessed uplights with low-wattage bulbs are a subtle way of marking out the pool edge for safety.

---

### SAFETY AROUND WATER

There are always areas in gardens where safety lighting is needed, but it can be achieved in a decorative manner. In modern gardens especially, it is particularly associated with decking and water (although not necessarily together). Although underwater lighting is not as common as you might expect, it is particularly important to mark the edge of a patio or deck so that an inattentive person does not take an unplanned swim. The same is true of stepping-stones and plank bridges over water. Recessed lights set into the walls of a swimming pool address this danger during nighttime parties around the pools and also allow others to see a swimmer in difficulty. Always use caution and consult a professional before installing underwater lights, as they are potentially hazardous.

**above:** Uplighting the trees and shrubs around a pool provides focal points and gives form to the area. The effect would have been improved if the fixtures were sunk into the ground so they couldn't be seen.

unseen obstacle, and task lighting will have reduced the risk of burns resulting from cooking on the barbecue in lower light levels. Beyond the specific lighting that is provided, the homeowners' knowledge of their own property provides them with added protection, or at least foreknowledge of hazards. For the visitor, good path and step lighting should illuminate hazards in unfamiliar territory. These might include places where the ground falls away at one side or where it would be easy to collide with a tree immediately to the side of the path, and entrances should be lit in a welcoming manner to show the most direct and safe way.

### Security lighting

For many people, security lighting is about deterrence, and the common solution, especially by security companies, is to install a floodlighting system triggered by passive infrared detectors that sense body heat and switch on the lighting when the heat source moves toward the building. The system is often zoned, so that floodlighting on different parts of the house can be monitored or switched on or off manually if required.

The ability to switch off such lighting is essential if you are going to invest in a subtle garden-lighting system and wish to avoid being blinded by floodlights every time you reach for a glass of wine. Many security experts now believe that this form of lighting is no deterrent to the determined professional thief but accept that it has a value in deterring casual would-be intruders and in providing homeowners with some reassurance that they have adopted the "appropriate measures" suggested by insurance companies.

The value of such protection is often reduced because the detectors are mounted on the house and so are activated only after the intruder has entered the property. This can be resolved by locating remote detectors and beam fences, but this strays into the world of the professional security specialist. Although technology has improved to avoid "false triggering," windblown branches and wildlife still cause lights to come on. This can be reduced by the choice of quality equipment and careful positioning of detectors, but false triggering will always be an occasional feature of such systems and can cause the homeowner anxiety about whether someone is lurking outside.

### Creating the illusion of occupation

Some homeowners prefer to use lighting to create the illusion that someone is at home. This usually involves lighting that comes on automatically at dusk and either stays on all night or is switched off by a timer when residents usually go to bed. This regular pattern of lighting makes it look as if the house is always occupied, especially if selected interior lighting operates in the same way. It is also possible for such lighting to switch on again automatically if movement is detected after the timer has switched off the lighting or to have panic buttons on the upper floors so that occupants can switch on the lighting if disturbing noises are heard. This form of security lighting often incorporates wall lights on the house, supplemented by lighting driveways and paths, but the garden's ornamental lighting circuits can also be incorporated into the scheme.

## Reassuring the homeowner

Security lighting makes the homeowner feel safer. This is partly based on the idea that good lighting is one of the best deterrents against intruders and partly on the belief that illuminated grounds offer a wider area of deterrence than an illuminated building. Bear in mind, however, that overly ostentatious front-garden lighting may draw your property to the attention of criminals.

One application of ornamental lighting becoming more common, especially in connection with crimes like mugging, is lighting shrub borders;

this offers reassurance that muggers are not hiding in wait when you return home from an evening out. At their most sophisticated, such schemes can extend to a lighting system that can be switched on from a remote control unit that also opens the gates and garage doors from inside the car.

**above left:** A twin PAR38 light with an integral passive infrared movement detector is an inexpensive but unattractive form of security lighting.

**below:** Patio spotlights can be timer-operated to provide an illusion of occupation when no one is at home.

# Garden-lighting effects

Having identified the areas in the garden that need lighting and the type of lighting that is required within them, it is time to turn to the different effects that can be achieved. A fine statue, positioned as a focal point at the end of a shrub border, will be lit in quite a different way from the interesting texture revealed on a house wall. Achieving these distinctive effects will require the use of the full range of lighting methods, which range from the comparatively straightforward techniques of uplighting and downlighting to the more subtle results that can be achieved by grazing, moon lighting and accent lighting.

## Downlighting

Lighting in a downward direction from a structure to provide a pool of light on a surface or feature below can provide general illumination for safety, security, and appearance, as well as a contrast to the uplighting of other features. Possibilities include downlighting from a pergola beam onto a dining table or path below, downward grazing and wall washing from under eaves, and spotlighting downward onto statues and other features (1). Downlighting is a useful way to illuminate flowering plants because flowers tend to face upward rather than downward; pergola-, wall- and tree-mounted fixtures can be used for this purpose.

Downlighting generally uses lower-power bulbs than uplighting because the applications tend to involve lighting downward toward the eye. Low-power bulbs with glare shields and internal glare louvres are widely used, while frosted

lenses are often used for diffused lighting around patios. For downlighting from pergolas, 20- or 35-watt halogen bulbs are usually used, while downlighting from trees or under eaves will require 50-watt bulbs only for the brightest applications.

## Uplighting

Lighting from below produces an effect that demands attention because it reverses the effect of daylight. The fixture should be aimed away from the viewpoint or shielded from view so that the beauty of the illuminated object can be appreciated without glare or the distraction of seeing where the lighting originates (2). Where there are multiple viewpoints, external glare shields or internal glare louvres help to achieve the required effect while reducing the glare in several directions.

**left:** Downlighting highlights the shape of topiary which would otherwise be hidden in shadow by uplighting from below.

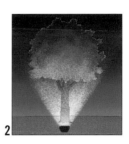

**below:** Two metal halide recessed uplights punch light up through the structure of this cedar. Ground mist reveals the light beams.

Uplighting is obviously the most common garden-lighting technique because ground-mounting is almost universally possible, whereas wall and overhead lighting platforms are not always available. Recessed uplights are recommended in flat areas where a spike-mounted light would be visually intrusive, a maintenance problem—mowing a lawn, for example—or a trip hazard—in paving on a terrace or porch. In other instances, spike-mounted uplights or spotlights are preferred because they are cheaper than recessed units and are more easily moved or adjusted to suit plant growth or seasonal changes.

Uplighting can produce a variety of effects, including accent lighting, washing, and grazing. It is used where special emphasis on a feature, such as a tree, statue, house facade, or wall, is required, but is also ideal for "infill" lighting of shrub borders to provide a visual link between individually illuminated features. Although we think of uplighting as a ground-based function, it can of course be achieved by spotlights mounted on walls, structures, and branches, and by underwater lights below the surface.

**right:** Uplighting adjacent shrubs and small trees places the illuminated statue in context with its surroundings.

**bottom:** Grazing light up the brick wall emphasizes its texture, particularly in contrast with the adjacent rendered walls.

1

### Grazing

Where texture is an obvious aspect of a feature or surface, lighting at an acute angle from a position near the surface will emphasize it by casting a strong shadow (1). The light is "grazing" the surface (although it is also sometimes

called "texturing") as well as emphasizing its color. An uplight placed close to the trunk of a tree will emphasize color, texture, and pattern in the bark, while the same uplight placed close to a columnar tree, such as a conifer, can be used to emphasize the textural appeal of the foliage.

A principal application is lighting stone or brick walls. Placing the fixture close to the wall will light the protruding surfaces and will throw the mortar joints and imperfections in the surface into sharp relief. While grazing a wall is often achieved by uplighting, it can also be achieved by downlighting from under eaves or from wall-mounted fixtures. When using step lights to light across steps or paved areas, the functional safety requirement is complemented by highlighting the decorative appeal of the color and texture of the building material.

## Washing

Providing an even coverage of light on a wall is called "washing" or "wall washing" and is used for many purposes. In modern gardens with painted, rendered walls lacking in texture, washing will draw attention to color or reflect from light walls to define the space and create an intimate atmosphere. The key to this effect in a small or intimate space is to use a low level of lighting, which contributes to a subtle ambience. The fixtures used may be surface- or ground-recessed and may feature either reflector bulbs—perhaps with frosted lenses to diffuse the light—or capsule bulbs within separate reflectors to provide diffused light (2). Manufacturers may use terms such as "wall washer" or "miniflood" for such fixtures.

Washing can also be used to light hedges or conifer screens to provide visual links or backdrops to individually lit features, such as statues or urns. On a larger scale, wall washing from ground-mounted floodlights can be used for facades, although you should bear in mind that this technique may cause glare when you glance out of a window or walk out through a doorway. Lighting the architectural features of the building in more selective ways produces better results in residential settings. A less common method of wall washing is to use small floodlights or diffuse downlights under the eaves of a house.

**top:** Washing light up the wall also outlines the containers and topiary. The stems and foliage of the climbers are also shadowed upward onto the surface.

would be visually flattened by frontal lighting to the point where the feature would appear as a flat cutout. Lighting from one side will often display this well, although this sometimes means that part of the form is lost in shadow. This can be rectified by adding another fixture on the opposite side, either a little further away or fitted with a less-bright bulb, so that infill lighting is sufficient to blank out part of the shadow without negating the textural effect of the first spotlight. spike-mounted fixtures will offer the most flexibility in balancing the lighting where two sources are used, but wall-mounted spotlights fixed to adjacent structures can be an effective alternative if you can choose from a wide enough range of bulbs.

**above:** Uplighting the statue from within the temple is complemented by crosslighting from the right which emphasizes the structure.

**right:** Crosslighting the statue of a lady from the right suits her shy pose as well as using shadow to reveal form.

Focused down the wall of the house, such fixtures can light the facade as well as the planting, entrance, and path areas below to provide security lighting.

## Crosslighting

Crosslighting is another term that describes the position of the fixture and the direction of light rather than the resulting lighting effect. It means placing the fixture to the side of the subject so that the light travels across it (1). Crosslighting a hedge by means of spotlights fitted with wide-beam bulbs can result in washing or grazing effects just as effectively as uplighting from directly in front.

Crosslighting is most often used where lighting from the side will emphasize texture and form more than lighting from the front. This is particularly useful where the form of a light-colored statue or relief on an urn

1

## Accent lighting

Accent lighting uses directional fixtures to emphasize individual plants, focal points, or other features so that they stand out within the view, either against a dark background or where a backdrop of a hedge, wall, or planting is less brightly illuminated. It can be achieved by any positional technique—uplighting, downlighting, or crosslighting—and from any point of origin—under water, in a tree, in the ground, or on a structure. It is achieved by focusing a relatively intense beam of light on the subject but requires careful positioning and aiming to avoid the evils of overlighting, which creates a washed-out appearance, or light spilling beyond the focal point to project ugly shadows on adjacent surfaces (2).

## Spotlighting

The term "spotlighting" is often confused with "accent lighting," and quite often it is the same thing. It usually refers to circumstances where the fixture is placed at some distance from the subject to be lit, often because there is no nearer practical mounting position (3). Examples could include spotlights under the eaves of a building used to illuminate focal points or paving features at ground level, or lighting the canopy of a tree from a planted border some distance from the trunk to avoid the use of a spike-mounted fixture in an intervening lawn area. Narrower, more intense "spotlight" beams may be used to compensate for the distance from the subject or to achieve a tight circle of light around the feature (see page 20).

**above:** A spike-mounted fixture accent lights the wall panel to reveal relief and provide a focal point through the dark foreground planting.

**below left:** Spotlighting down onto an architectural plant creates a stunning focal point, an effect accentuated by leaving the surrounding planting in darkness.

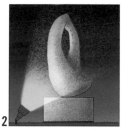

2

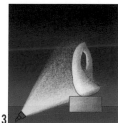

3

## Mirroring

Mirroring is achieved quite simply by accent lighting a feature on the far side of a body of water so that its image is mirrored in the water when it is seen from a viewpoint on the patio, in the house or from a strategically placed seat (1). The best subjects are those with a light color and clear outline reflected in sharp focus on the water—for example, simple urns and classical features, such as a stone temple.

Mirroring is a simple matter of geometry. If an object is illuminated, the mirroring effect will be achieved as long as the body of water is large enough to accommodate the size of the reflection from a given viewpoint. Because it

**right:** Light-colored focal points make good subjects for mirroring in formal ponds.

**below:** Mirroring of these busts of Bacchus and a Bacchae in the dark water of the swimming pool is a creative alternative to leaving the pool lighting on.

depends as much on the angle of view as it does on the size of the subject, it can even be achieved on a miniature scale on a roof garden. The mirroring will succeed only if the subject is brightly illuminated and the water is sufficiently dark. For example, a tree with a fairly dense canopy must be both uplit and receive external canopy lighting; uplighting from within the canopy is likely to be too subtle to reflect strongly in the water. The lighting must be bright enough to outweigh any moonlight or glow from city lights on the surface of the water, and stray light from interior illumination or area lighting near the water must be eliminated. Underwater lighting should be avoided and lighting of adjacent areas limited in brightness. See also page 62.

1

## Silhouetting

This effect occurs when a dark image of a subject is created by lighting a wall or other vertical surface behind it. While the color and texture of the subject are hidden, the interesting shape of a small tree, an architectural plant, or an object with a distinctive outline can make a fascinating focal point. An alternative is where screening plants are "silhouetted" against a pale wall to produce a textured tableau: bamboos are particularly good subjects for this treatment. Wide diffused beams, as used in straightforward wall washing, will give the best result. Occasionally, the effect comes not from garden lighting but from interior lighting silhouetting the exterior planting against the illuminated background of plain blinds, or perhaps "shoji" screens in a Japanese context to provide a pleasing backdrop to a terrace. Courtyards can benefit from this effect.

## The halo effect

You may have read descriptions of backlighting trees to produce a silhouette effect, but this is a misinterpretation of the word "silhouette" (see left). If there is no illuminated background, there is no silhouette. What backlighting does is produce a halo of light around the edges of the trunk and branches in the case of a spreading tree or the foliage outline in the case of a conifer (2). The halo shows the shape or structure of the tree and is a subtle effect against a dark background. The halo treatment is often used where there is a need to provide variety among other trees and shrubs that are lit more from the front or side. If the lighting comes from directly behind the subject, the effect may be too subtle to have any impact. It is often better to place the fixture behind and slightly to one side of the tree to produce a more pronounced halo effect on one side. It works better

**below left:** Uplighting the wall from behind the urn throws the phormium into silhouette against the background of textured brickwork.

2

above: Low-level lighting around the balcony leaves the eye free to appreciate the vista.

below: Downlighting from between overhead beams is a subtle way of lighting an area for relaxation if the light sources are both obscured from view and limited in power.

where light filtering up through translucent foliage, such as that of some maples, adds a more colorful effect.

## Area lighting

The function of area lighting is to provide sufficient general illumination within an area so that it is possible to do whatever activity is appropriate. It is the principal method of providing the

kind of lighting we regard as essential in an outdoor room. On a patio that might include lighting to eat or read by, to help us navigate around the table and toys, and to carry food and utensils to and from the table. Directional lighting can be used for some of these activities if there is an overhead beam to mount such fixtures on, but it can be intrusive unless done well.

We are also accustomed to area lighting around us when we are in the dining and living rooms, either directly from wall or ceiling fixtures or indirectly by reflection from the surrounding surfaces, and we carry this expectation with us when we go outside. It is sometimes referred to as "ambient lighting," although strictly speaking ambient light in the garden at night is the sum of moonlight plus light from the sky in a city or at dusk. The point is that in the garden setting, area lighting should be sufficiently soft, diffuse, and flattering to create an ambience that is subtle, relaxing, and perhaps a little romantic.

Unless ornamental techniques such as moon lighting from trees or wall washing from under the eaves of the

house are feasible, area lighting is generally achieved by the use of line-voltage, wall-mounted lights on the house or on other adjacent walls, sometimes built for that purpose. These may be supplemented by column-mounted lights or by low-level lighting from spread lights.

### Floodlighting

Floodlighting is, of course, the ultimate type of area lighting, designed to mimic the high power and bland spread of daylight (1). It is often misused to light horizontally from the house, to the annoyance of neighbors and astronomers. Its main application in residential premises is security lighting, where 300- to 500-watt halogen units are not uncommon. These are unnecessarily high wattages for most residential applications, particularly if they are badly focused and directed, and 150 watts is more than adequate for many domestic applications. A bit of thought about their location and focusing can make them an asset rather than a nuisance. Using small, 100- to 150-watt halogen floodlights or 50-watt wide-beam downlights under the eaves of a two-

story house can provide adequate security lighting as well as washing the facade and lighting the planting, path, and entrance below. Floodlights should be focused downward within an angle of sixty degrees from vertical to avoid light trespass and glare to neighboring properties, paths, or roads.

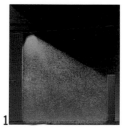

**top:** Downlighting from garden structures produces more subtle effects than floodlighting from house walls.

**left:** Interior lighting reflects from the overhead canopy to provide diffuse illumination for viewers of this cityscape.

**right:** Recessed step lighting provides safe access without excessive visual intrusion into the surface finish.

**below right:** A louvred stainless steel recessed light adds a modern touch to glare-free step lighting.

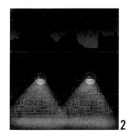

## Step and vista lighting

Step lighting is a functional requirement rather than a lighting technique, but it merits separate consideration as it provides a convenient heading to discuss the discreet lighting of steps and the horizontal surfaces to or from which they lead. Where overhead lighting is not an available option, lighting at step level becomes necessary. Each individual tread should receive direct lighting, unshadowed by the riser above, from light sources shielded within the fixture so the pedestrian is not blinded or distracted by glare while ascending the stairs (1).

Fixtures fixed in the risers of steps will be directly in the line of vision as your eyes check the route forward for your feet to follow, but this is sometimes the only available option—where there is no flanking wall, bank, or balustrade, for example, or on circular staircases. It is better to provide step lighting through small lights set into, or mounted on, a flanking wall. Choose

types that are characterized by shields, grilles, inset bulb housings, or "eyelid" hoods that hide the light source from passing overhead view.

Step lighting can also be useful when it is important to protect a vista—for example, when foreground lighting of steps, patio (2), or deck must be directed downward so that it does not make it impossible to see a view beyond.

## Spread lighting

Manufacturers use the terms "spread light" or "path light" for their products, while consumers tend to call them "mushroom lights." Spread lighting is the use of low-level fixtures to provide a glare-free, usually circular pool of light for a path, step, patio, or area of low planting (3). They commonly have halogen bulbs or halogen capsule bulbs of around 20 watts and provide a circle of light 8–13 feet across. In many ways, spread lighting is a last resort because the fixtures must be visible if they are to do their job. However, where

ornamental lighting techniques such as moon lighting cannot be used and where there are no walls or structures on which to mount recessed or discreet lights, spread lights must be used to fulfill essential safety functions in lighting path and steps, as well as to fill in areas of darkness.

**left:** Spread lights are a matter of taste and a last resort for path lighting. Choosing colors that blend in among planting makes them more acceptable.

**bottom:** Copper spread lights provide pools of light around decking and low planting. Weathered copper blends well with timber and gravel.

3

1

## Shadowing

The shadow of a plant or small tree can be projected onto a wall behind by placing a spotlight in front of the plant so that the light shines through the foliage toward the wall (1). This simple technique uses a low-power, wide-beam bulb in a spike-mounted spotlight, typically 20–35 watts. Vary the distance between the light source and the object being lit to alter the size of the image that is projected on the wall. Shadowing is an easy way of achieving maximum effect from a small tree in a newly planted courtyard garden, and may also be used to cast the shadow of water spray from a fountain.

Shadowing is usually directed at a vertical surface and its potential for paving is often overlooked. Using wall-mounted spotlights to cast the shadow of climbing plants or plants in containers is a way of adding dappled interest on paving in the smallest of gardens. A more novel use is to position discreet spotlights on fencing, a trellis, or a pergola to cast light down through

architectural planting to provide shadow-enriched path or patio lighting.

## Moon lighting

Trees can be excellent lighting platforms for illuminating all manner of garden features and areas below, including herbaceous and shrub borders, terraces, lawns, driveways, paths, steps, and seating areas. A favorite technique is "moon lighting" down from low-power lights fixed in a tree to shadow the lower branches and foliage onto the ground below (2). This provides a wonderfully subtle, dappled, lighting effect over a tree seat and is also a creative way of integrating the lawn into the lighting scene. In a small garden, a halogen spotlight suspended from a branch about 16 feet above the ground with a 35-watt, 60-degree bulb would be a good choice. For denser foliage or higher mounting points, move up to a 50-watt bulb, but for smaller trees reduce the power to 20 watts.

If the light source is positioned

| USING MOON LIGHTING | |
|---|---|
| **SUBJECT TO BE LIT** | **EFFECT OF MOON LIGHTING** |
| **Planted urns** | Reveals planting, while uplighting illuminates the urns below. |
| **Seating areas** | Dappled light over alfresco dining area, tree seat, or bench creates a romantic atmosphere. |
| **Driveways** | Textured lighting adds interest to adjacent planting and features. |
| **Lawns and graveled areas** | Emphasizes horizontal dimensions in a natural way. |
| **Water features** | Makes moving water sparkle; casts a silvery sheen onto pools; provides safety. |
| **Structures** | Reveals roof shapes and tiling; provides shadow-enriched lighting through an open structure. |
| **Paths and steps** | Provides natural-looking safety lighting; illuminates features along the way. |
| **Planting** | Displays upward-facing flowers; provides contrast to uplighting; illuminates borders in a natural way. |
| **Statues** | Illuminates upward-facing subjects that uplighting would leave in shadow. |

**2**

20–23 feet above ground, maintenance may become more difficult, so discharge light sources (metal halide or mercury vapor) are usually preferred because of their longer bulb life. Using "cooler" discharge bulbs of 4000–4500K color temperature will also give you the slightly blue light of true moonlight, an effect you can also achieve with halogen fixtures by inserting a pale blue filter.

It is especially important to ensure that fittings are high enough above a walkway or seating area and not so bright as to invite an upward glance, which will only perceive glare. Internal honeycomb louvres can help to shield the light source from view, and glare guards are essential for fixtures directed away from the trunk. In the latter case, fittings must be directed downward, within a maximum of 30 degrees angle from the vertical to avoid glare toward viewpoints or neighbors.

Moon lighting from a tree should be accompanied by uplighting of the trunk to anchor the tree to the ground, avoiding an impression of glowing foliage floating above the ground. This combination plays down the sources of light in the tree to a pleasing glow in the canopy where the uplighting and downlighting beams meet. Where the lights are located below the lowest branches, the effect is downlighting to apply a wash of light, rather than dappled light, onto the area below.

### MOON LIGHTING SMALL AREAS

In small gardens, and even on balconies and roof gardens, the moon lighting effect can be imitated by placing spotlights on walls or structures above climbers or planted urns so that the foliage's shadow falls onto the ground below.

# Lighting
# garden features

Of all the features in the garden, water is the one that most invites the use of lighting. Still, dark pools, rippling streams, or cascading fountains and waterfalls present unparalleled opportunities for the creative and subtle use of light. Individual plants are also ideal subjects for lighting, whether it is the graceful form of an upright tree or the large, dramatic foliage of a shrub or perennial. Few gardens have no structures that can be lit—pergolas and arbors, for example, are possible subjects. The structure and architecture of the house itself can be lit to emphasize striking features or disguise less attractive ones.

## Water features

Whether moving or still, water always takes center stage in a garden-lighting scheme. The trickling water of a stream, the rush of a waterfall, the sparkle of a fountain, and the sheen of light on still water are all mesmerizing in their own ways. At night, water contributes a magical range to the palette of garden-lighting effects, for, if creative garden lighting is about painting with light, then water provides the most varied of canvases. Remember, however, that electricity can be hazardous, particularly where water is involved, so take proper precautions and hire a professional for installation.

### Moving water

Some applications involve uplighting from still water, but these tend to be the exception. The main interests in lighting lie in exploiting two properties of water—refraction and reflection. Refraction is the property by which light is bent as it passes through the surface of water. It poses no real problems for lighting upward from under still water because the fixture can be simply adjusted to point the beam in the right direction. If the surface of the water is moving—because it is disturbed by a nearby waterfall or the cascade from a fountain, for example—the refraction at the water surface is continuously varied

and the light coming up through the moving water is similarly varied, the light beam being bent at random, producing a shimmering lighting effect. If we light a wall fountain, in particular, the whole scene becomes one of light dancing on the wall, the fountain, and any adjacent planting.

### Still water

The reflection of a statue, focal point, or specimen tree in dark, still water can create a stunning but tranquil scene. It involves a relatively simple technique and can be applied to any swimming pool, lake, or smaller pond. Lighting a strongly outlined subject or architectural feature on the far side of the pool produces an image that is reflected on the water in the foreground. This is also a very creative way of using a body of water that cannot itself be lit.

### Complex water features

Water features that combine many different lighting opportunities within one area are found only in larger gardens. Within a complex design many ideas that are individually

above: Commercial landscape lighting techniques, including "glitter" lighting of structures and colorful underwater lighting of water features, are inappropriate for most residential settings.

left: Underwater uplighting in a ring around the fountain catches the sparkling water falling from the fountain bowl. Crosslighting from outside the water feature reveals the upper features.

above: Complex lighting in and around this large pond includes underwater uplighting of waterfalls, lighting of planting that is reflected in darker areas of water, and underlighting the bridge. The overall effect is perhaps a little fussy and overly bright.

applicable to a wide range of features come together. Sophisticated lighting design is achieved by looking at individual parts and the appropriate lighting effects and then by integrating them into a complete design.

### Underwater lighting

Underwater uplighting of moving water, for example, a simple waterfall or fountain using a waterproof underwater spotlight, is a common and effective technique. Glistening water and the shimmering light projected by underwater lighting through moving water can be fascinating. The light adds the dimension of movement to otherwise still surfaces around the central cascade, and, even where there is no feature operated by a submersible pump, the rippling of water by the wind can be enough to provide interesting movement.

### Fountains

Where a fountain is only a gush of water propelled upward by an underwater jet, the foaming water is the feature to be lit. Positioning an underwater light immediately next to the source of the water spout will make sure that it is lit while concealing the light source within the luminescence of the foaming water. Often, however, a fountain is more than just the sparkle of falling water: the origin of the water flow may be a statue or another ornamental feature rather than just a piece of copper pipe. In that case, the design needs to adopt some of the principles of statue lighting, particularly the need to avoid strong shadows that occur when lighting upward from too close to the feature.

Another consideration may apply with regard to tiered fountains. Lighting a fall of water from a basin into the base pool is only part of the job;

left: The "sunburst" wall fountain provides a perfect focus for lighting upward from the cobblestone-filled basin.

lighting the statue or feature that fills the upper tier basin may require the bulbs to be moved to the edge of the lower pool in order to maximize the coverage of the upper feature. In larger tiered fountains it may be necessary to use two sets of fixtures. One will uplight the fall of water from the upper basin, the other will sit on the outer edge of the base pool or within the upper basin to light the feature from which the water flow originates. In most fountaina, 35- to 50-watt bulbs are the norm.

### Wall fountains

The need to avoid heavy shadow also applies in lighting wall-mask fountains, so avoid placing the fixtures underneath the water spout. The ideal technique is to position the fixture with a narrow- or medium-beam bulb so that light appears to travel up the water spout to accent the mask against the surrounding surface. Alternatively, a wider-beam bulb in a fixture mounted further to the front of the basin or pool below may be used as a compromise to avoid ugly shadows. While wider beam bulbs may be preferred for wall masks mounted on ornamental walls or to produce a wider area of shimmering light from below moving water, narrower beams will emphasize the water flow and mask.

For larger wall fountains or those that feature several spouts, the approach can be more complex. Accent lighting of individual spouts while using lower-power, wider-beam bulbs for an overall wash can be effective. Provided the lights sit reasonably close to the surface of the water, 20-watt bulbs should be powerful enough to illuminate most wall fountains.

below: Uplighting from the lower pool is complemented by lighting of the upper feature from inside the tiered basin.

**right:** Uplighting the plank walls and timber structures provides an architectural framework for recessed crosslighting of this azure lagoon. The sheet of falling water receives light from the fixtures recessed into the decking, as well as from underwater lighting in front.

bridge often provides sufficient illumination to define the positions of the horizontal pathway, vertical structure, and water's edge. Obvious surface-mounted lights on the bridge structure are ugly, although small copper spotlights can often be acceptable because they weather attractively to blend with timber structures. Alternatively, spiking a spotlight into the bank close to each end of a bridge can light the structure well. Setting the lights at an acute angle will usually hide the light source from view as pedestrians cross the bridge, while using glare guards and internal glare louvres will control glare on the approaches to the bridge.

If walkway lighting is required, products that can light under a handrail or from the interior uprights can be used, but these need to be carefully positioned so they do not protrude into the walkway or intrude into the daylight view of the bridge. Sometimes spotlights mounted under the bridge shine down onto, beneath, and around the water, and this can certainly be attractive where there are interesting rocks or plants to flatter the water area below. Take care to ensure that light bounced off the water surface does not become glare from another viewpoint. Although lighting emphasizes sparkle in water, sparkle and glare are two sides of the same coin, and light reflecting

off sheets of water can sometimes be unpredictable. Moon lighting from waterside trees is a better and more natural-looking way of lighting routes around and over water.

## Waterfalls

Waterfalls offer a timeless fascination in the natural landscape and lose none of their appeal when they are mimicked, even in unnatural interpretations, in our own gardens. Whether the water flows over a rocky precipice in a tumbling cascade or flows in a shimmering sheet over a metal chute or the flat edge of machined slate, the sparkle and luminescence as it falls into a basin below demand emphasis by lighting at night. The underwater spotlight is usually best located immediately below the entry point of the cascade of the water into the pool beneath so that it will be shielded among the foaming luminescence while the light beam is directed up the flow of water to create prismatic effects.

If lighting is placed in front of the waterfall, it tends to pass through the flow and light the area behind it without picking up the essential sparkle of the water; and, if the flow is a sheet of smooth water, lighting from the front might just bounce off the water "mirror" at an angle to cause unpredictable glare. Where there is an interesting rock formation behind the waterfall, moving the fixture slightly behind the cascade can create the illusion of a rock grotto with a sparkling curtain in front. Underwater fixtures must be mounted on brackets, which can be tightened to maintain focus, and fixed on secure supports, which can withstand buffeting from water turbulence. The support must be moveable so that the optimum position can be achieved and so that the fixture can be removed from the water for occasional bulb-changing and maintenance. Even in the cleanest water feature there will be a certain amount of encrustation resulting from waterborne salts and algae; this will have to be removed from time to time.

### Rock gardens

Rock gardens are frequently found alongside waterfalls, and they can form the backdrop to the focal point of the waterfall. By their nature, rock gardens recede from the water's edge, with a sheer area of rock constructed for the main event—the water dropping

**above:** Underwater uplighting of the waterfalls is complemented by infill lighting of the rocks and planting, which can't be reached by underwater fixtures.

down the face. The receding levels of the rocks mean that any underwater light placed to uplight the waterfall from below will merely cast the upper rocks—and any planting at the upper levels—into complete shadow. The solution is to place extra spotlights around the lower pool and sides of the rock feature so that they will either provide lower-level infill lighting of areas cast into shadow by the underwater lighting, or light planting and additional ornaments as secondary focal points.

Whichever blend of secondary or supplementary lighting is appropriate, the direction and intensity of the lighting should not compete with the waterfall as the primary focal point, nor should it blank out the light that shimmers on the rock face. This may seem expensive, but the low-budget approach of placing a powerful, wide-beam bulb at the front of the pool to light the waterfall and rocks in one fell swoop will simply result in a boring, flat scene relieved only by a small bit of sparkle.

### Streams

Streams can make beautiful illuminated features. A meandering stream will enhance a moonlight walk and contrast with a raised deck or other linear feature. Planning the lighting in advance of construction can be difficult because the final look of the feature will owe much to the positioning of the rocks, falls, and planting, and to the skill of the landscape contractor in creating a natural-looking landscape. Planning for a network of cable ducts under the stream will make it easier to finalize the lighting design once the rocks, pools, and falls are seen in reality rather than on a plan.

Stream features can lack the depth of water in which to hide underwater lighting, so remote lighting techniques are often used. Moon lighting from trees is a good option because it is a natural-looking effect and removes the difficulty

---

### CAMOUFLAGING FIXTURES AROUND WATER FEATURES

It is far less easy to light a stream when there are no trees to act as lighting platforms for the moon lighting effect. Nothing spoils the naturalistic effect of a stream feature more than visible light fixtures, so close attention to camouflaging the positions of the fixtures is paramount. Using step lights mounted on low flanking walls or tucked under the edge of decking may be one way of hiding the light sources. If ground-mounted lights are used, small, green, spike-mounted spotlights (with glare guards if they are near a pathway) may be hidden among streamside planting to light an area of rock, a pool, a cluster of marginal

planting, or a small waterfall where there is insufficient depth for an underwater light. These provide points of emphasis, either used alone or to blend with moonlight if the feature consists of a succession of focal points. A series of 20-watt, wide-beam, halogen bulbs, perhaps with frosted lenses to diffuse the beams in close-up lighting situations, works best.

Where spike-mounting is not possible because there is a butyl liner, wedging waterproof lights among flanking rocks is another alternative, possibly using cast brass or bronze fixtures, which will weather to blend in with rocky surroundings. If there is no diffused lighting from trees, other means of infill lighting will be needed to link any spotlit areas. This might involve low-power, probably 20-watt, halogen mini-floodlights mounted on stakes hidden in adjacent planting areas. As a last resort, it might involve using spreadlights to provide circular pools of light, although stem-mounted path lights with a 180-degree distribution would be better, provided you can camouflage the fixtures. These cast light gently across an area, while leaving the area behind in darkness.

of hiding ground-mounted fixtures and ensuring that they produce no directional glare. The effect produced by moon lighting is both widespread and diffused, so the lighting is not patchy and represents good value for a gardener working with a limited budget. Most importantly, it produces a silvery sheen on the surface of stiller water.

**Small water features**

The bubbling of water can add a certain something to even the smallest garden, whether it is a courtyard, balcony, or roof garden. At night, lighting brings an intimacy to such areas that is much more difficult to achieve in many larger settings. In this sort of setting, glittering water acts as a magnet to the eye. Small features should be subtly lit to suit their size.

**above:** Lighting a meandering stream will add interest to an evening walk.

## Upright water features

If it is upright, uplight it. Following this simple rule is usually the best approach because the vertical dimension should be emphasized to enhance the effect of the moving water. Small water features of this kind, such as cobblestone fountains, are often prefabricated and have a small base reservoir. Water drops onto a cobblestone, flint, or pebble layer that masks a supporting grid over the reservoir. This cosmetic layer over the grid is ideal for hiding a waterproof uplight: perhaps a black one with slate, or a brass one that will age to blend in among the cobblestones. In most situations, 20-watt bulbs will be sufficient, and you may need to use an internal glare louvre if the feature is close to a patio or window.

To uplight urn water features, where the water trickles down the side of the urn to be recirculated and pumped back up inside, an underwater light inside the urn is sometimes used to provide shimmering uplighting on an overhead

**above:** Underwater uplighting of the waterfall produces shimmering illumination of the brick structure, while crosslighting of the water staircase adds a sparkling sheen to the trickling of the water running down.

**right:** Illumination of the wall feature leaves unlit planting to frame the view with silhouettes.

canopy. However, uplighting the trickling water on the outside is more effective. Do not place the light too close to the side of the urn or you will get a "dinner plate" of light, as the beam does not have the opportunity to spread. Position the light a little way back, use the widest beam bulb available, and fit a frosted lens to diffuse the beam. A "spread" lens is a useful device that will turn a circular beam into an elongated oval or rectangle to help with lighting taller or wider objects from close range.

### Low water features

Small, low-water features are best lit from above or the side. If there is an overhead or adjacent structure, focus a surface-mounted spotlight with a 20- to 35-watt bulb in a narrow to medium beam spread on it. This will provide accent lighting that will make the feature stand out from its surroundings, while leaving adjacent surfaces, such as fences, which you do not necessarily want to light, in the dark. A 50-watt, narrow or very narrow beam may be needed to spotlight the feature from a more distant mounting point, such as under the eaves of the house.

If no overhead lighting position exists, spread lighting may be the next best choice. However, if possible, use a 180-degree, path-lighting product to diffuse light toward the feature while disguising the source of the light. The use of pole-mounted spotlights works only if the fixtures can be disguised.

Water features, such as millstones, urns, or fountains, can be downlit from a wall or pergola, or illuminated by a spread light or area lighting source tucked into adjacent planting. For example, using a copper light with a very small head and a shield to restrict the lighting to a 180-degree arc allows a low-level subject to be lit without light being projected toward a viewpoint. Where you need a ground-level light source that diffuses light rather than projecting a beam, especially if the available lighting position is close to the subject, a spike-mounted spread light, step light, or a miniature low-voltage floodlight mounted on a short stake are options to consider.

**above:** Underwater uplighting of the fountain from several directions makes this striking feature a fitting focal point in the center of the courtyard.

---

## SAFETY AROUND WATER

Water is a potential hazard in the garden, especially around electricity, so be sure you check with an expert before you embark on a project. The electricity supply used for pumps and filters as well as for lighting must have proper circuit protection, and all transformers should have secondary fuse protection. However, lighting has an important role to play in promoting the safe use of water features at night. Lighting the body of water from beneath to show where firm ground ends is one option. In addition, lighting paths, bridges, stepping-stones, and banks so that the water's edge and safe routes around or across the feature are clearly visible is an essential safety requirement.

## Trees

A tree provides a unique opportunity to add vertical emphasis and drama to the evening landscape, and illuminated trees can produce stunning results, adding scale to the nightscape whether they are primary features, seen directly or mirrored in the dark water of a pond or lake, or secondary features, acting as backdrops to a statue or formal feature.

### Lighting techniques

Uplighting is the most common technique used for lighting trees, but the position and type of light fixture and choice of bulb type and power can produce varying results. You need to assess the tree's size, canopy density, structure, shape, color, textures, and position. There are more choices possible for the type of bulb and lighting than for almost any other subject in the garden.

Deciding which trees to light and which techniques to use requires careful consideration. Lighting large trees close to an exterior viewpoint, such as the patio, may have a majestic impact if the fixture can be shielded from view. However, the same tree close to the house may be difficult to see easily from a window. Conversely, small trees some distance from the house may be seen only as a blob of light from a window. The farther a tree is from the viewpoint, the more brightly it must be lit if it is not to fade into the distance, while closer subjects catch your eye instead.

### Choosing subjects to light

Just because a particular tree is a favorite, it does not necessarily mean that it is a good candidate for lighting, because any structural faults will be glaringly obvious. Light the side that is not wind-damaged, for example, or light it less brightly than other subjects in the garden so that it becomes a secondary focal point.

An alternative is to use it as a lighting platform to moon light down onto the ground, transferring attention to a lawn, patio, or feature below (see

pages 52–53). Remember that it is still important to uplight the trunk of a tree to some extent to tie it to the ground or the moon lighting may make the canopy appear to hover in midair.

In some gardens there may be many specimens vying for attention. Do not be tempted to light them all, or to light many of them in the same way. Pick out a few really good specimens and go for contrast. Light them from the front or different sides, or use different lighting intensities or bulb color temperatures to reinforce the different foliage. Equally, do not try for variety where none should exist; an avenue of

**far right:** The translucent leaves of *Acer palmatum* 'Bloodgood' will glow a brilliant red as light filters upward from a 50-watt uplight situated below.

**right:** Laburnum flowers bloom for a short time and make a stunning spectacle under lighting, but you may wish to focus the spotlight on more interesting companion planting for the rest of the year.

trees can only be lit as an avenue of trees—uniformly—unless you are attempting the dangerous game of trying to create false perspectives.

**Tree color**

The color of a tree will be an important consideration when you are selecting lighting, but it is even more important for smaller, ornamental trees in smaller gardens, where the overwhelming grandeur of a larger tree is not the prime factor. Some good specimen trees are listed on pages 70–71, together with the characteristics that make them appropriate for lighting.

There are a few general guidelines to bear in mind.

Light-colored foliage, bark, flowers, or berries will always stand out with relatively low-powered lighting. The same is true for trees with colorful, translucent leaves, especially if they are red or orange, such as some maples and sweet gum trees in autumn. Avoid overlighting these subjects, or the effect may be overpowering; choose fixtures that you can trade down to a lower-wattage bulb if necessary. Darker foliage and bark may need at least two to three times as much lighting as light-colored subjects for the same sort of

**above:** Moon lighting down through the open structure of a deciduous tree throws a strong shadow of the branch structure onto the ground below. Uplighting of the trunk could link the two areas together more positively.

| TREES FOR LIGHTING | |
|---|---|
| **TREE** | **CHARACTERISTICS AS A GOOD LIGHTING SUBJECT** |
| *Acer capillipes*<br>Snake bark maple | Striped bark and bright green leaves, which turn brilliant orange and red in autumn |
| *Acer japonicum* 'Aconitifolium'<br>Full-moon maple | Elegant habit and deeply dissected leaves, which turn ruby-red or crimson in autumn |
| *Acer negundo* 'Variegatum'<br>Ash-leaved box maple | Fast-growing, small to medium-sized tree with green leaves with white edges |
| *Acer palmatum* 'Bloodgood'<br>Japanese maple | Deep reddish-purple translucent leaves make a fiery spectacle when uplit |
| *Acer platanoides* 'Drummondii'<br>Harlequin maple | Striking, large tree with large green leaves with a broad, creamy white margin |
| *Acer saccharinum*<br>Silver maple | Deeply divided, light green leaves with silver undersides turn butter yellow in autumn |
| *Alnus glutinosa* 'Imperialis'<br>Alder | Lovely cultivar with deeply divided leaves |
| *Arbutus unedo*<br>Strawberry tree | Small tree with dark evergreen leaves, white flowers and red "strawberry" fruit |
| *Betula pendula* 'Laciniata'<br>European white birch | Tall, slender tree with a silvery bark, pendulous branches, and deeply cut leaves |
| *Betula pendula* 'Youngii'<br>Young's weeping birch | Graceful, umbrella-shaped, weeping tree with attractive foliage and white bark |
| *Carpinus betulus* 'Fastigiata'<br>Hornbeam | Medium-sized tree; the columnar shape broadens to almost round as it matures |
| *Castanea sativa* 'Albomarginata'<br>Spanish chestnut | Fast-growing, large tree with long, toothed, shiny green leaves with white margins |
| *Catalpa bignonioides*<br>Indian bean tree | Umbrella-shaped tree with large, heart-shaped leaves and white and purple flowers |
| *Cedrus libani* subsp. *libani*<br>Cedar of Lebanon | Open structure with horizontal branches and tufts of dark green needles |
| *Cercidiphyllum japonicum*<br>Katsura tree | Medium-sized tree, usually grown for its autumn color |
| *Cornus controversa* 'Variegata'<br>Giant dogwood | Beautiful small tree with horizontal branches of pendulous green and white leaves |
| *Cryptomeria japonica* Elegans Group<br>Japanese cedar | Elegant conifer with brownish-green curving leaves, which turn coppery bronze in autumn |
| *Cupressus sempervirens* Stricta Group<br>Italian cypress | Tall, slim, dark green columns, most effective when grouped to form living sculptures |
| *Fagus sylvatica* 'Dawyck'<br>Dawyck beech | Columnar form of the European beech; the bronze-leaved form is *F. s.* 'Dawyck's Purple' |

| SPECIMEN TREES | |
| --- | --- |
| **TREE** | **CHARACTERISTICS AS A GOOD LIGHTING SUBJECT** |
| *Fagus sylvatica* 'Pendula'<br>Weeping beech | Dramatic weeping tree with autumn color |
| *Fraxinus diversifalia* 'Pendula'<br>Weeping ash | In winter the downwash of weeping branches turns the tree into a living sculpture |
| *Gleditsia triacanthos* 'Sunburst'<br>Honey locust | Fern-like, glossy golden-yellow foliage in spring |
| *Ilex aquifolium* 'Argentea Marginata'<br>English holly | Shiny variegated leaves reflect light brilliantly |
| *Laburnum alpinum* 'Pendulum'<br>Scotch laburnum | Weeping branches are spectacular with hanging racemes of yellow flowers |
| *Ligustrum lucidum* 'Tricolor'<br>Chinese privet | Evergreen tree with glossy green leaves with creamy white edges and creamy white flowers |
| *Liquidambar styraciflua*<br>Sweetgum | Conical tree with glossy leaves that turn purple, orange, and red in autumn |
| *Liriodendron tulipifera* 'Fastigiatum'<br>Upright tulip tree | Columnar when young, turning more ovoid with age; large green leaves turning gold in autumn |
| *Paulownia tomentosa*<br>Foxglove tree | Open branches carry clusters of heliotrope-blue, foxglove-like flowers in spring |
| *Populus x candicans* 'Aurora'<br>Balm of Gilead | Large, balsam-scented green leaves boldly variegated with pink-tinged, cream blotches |
| *Prunus serrula*<br>Cherry | Polished mahogany-colored bark |
| *Prunus x yedoensis* 'Shidare-yoshino'<br>Potomac cherry | Graceful spreading tree with hanging branches covered with blossom in early spring |
| *Pyrus salicifolia* 'Pendula'<br>Willow-leaved pear | Weeping branches of silvery foliage |
| *Robinia pseudoacacia* 'Umbraculifera'<br>Black locust | Naturally rounded shape and soft, light green foliage |
| *Salix babylonica* var. *pekinensis* 'Tortuosa'<br>Dragon-claw willow | Small tree with twisting stems and pendulous leaves that turn yellow in autumn |
| *Salix caprea* 'Kilmarnock'<br>Kilmarnock willow | Weeping tree with silky male catkins |
| *Sorbus vilmorinii*<br>Ash tree | Arching branches with clusters of blue-green, fern-like leaves turning red-purple in autumn |
| *Taxus baccata* 'Fastigiata'<br>Irish yew | Strong, upright shape; the golden form is *T. b.* 'Aurea' |

effect, and if you want to light a copper beech or purple sycamore be prepared to use five times (or more) as much lighting power. Even then, you will not see much of the very dark foliage. Instead, try to exploit its darkness by lighting up through the center of the tree so that the dark foliage is silhouetted against the inner glow. Rather than trying for the same lighting effect on very different subjects, light them to emphasize their differences and make a feature of the contrast.

If the tree's glory is short-lived, make sure that the tree is at least acceptable in the lighting scene for the rest of the year. Apple blossoms and the yellow flowers of laburnum may be stunning for a while, but will such trees still look good under lighting for the rest of the year? In some cases, refocusing the spotlight on companion planting provides an opportunity to ring the changes. In other cases, explore alternative concepts as well: can the orchard become a moonlit walk, for example? Always keep the direction and distance of the viewpoint in mind; uplighting trees for interesting bark color or texture is worthwhile only if they are close enough to a viewpoint for it to be appreciated. If they are not, work with the shape and canopy to grab the attention instead.

### Tree shape

The power of the light source and whether it is focused into a narrow or wide beam will determine how far up the tree the light can travel (see page 76). The key question is whether the structure of the tree and the density of the canopy will prevent the light from reaching this far. Stand back and assess the tree's shape and geometry and whether it limits the possible positions of one or more uplights: are there large roots, surrounding paving, nearby water, or

---

### UPLIGHTING TREES
### SHAPE AND STRUCTURE

The method of lighting trees depends principally on shape and structure, as shown below by: a tree with an open structure, a tree with a dense canopy, a textured tree with a dense canopy, and a mature tree with an open structure.

**1.** Trees with an open structure and canopy can be uplit, using spike-mounted uplights hidden among planting or recessed lights in a lawn. Emphasis on structure.

**2.** Trees with a dense canopy and attractive shape must be lit from outside the canopy. Use a spike-mounted wide-beam spotlight or floodlight located in an adjacent border. Emphasis on shape.

**3.** Trees with a densely textured canopy can be "grazed" by uplighting near the outside of the canopy. Use a spike-mounted spotlight or adjustable recessed uplight with a narrow to medium beam. Emphasis on texture.

**4.** Large, mature trees with open structure and dense foliage require uplighting the trunk with a narrow beam and the canopy with one or more under beams. Emphasis on structure.

simply directions from which the tree must, or must not, be viewed? Remember that halogen bulb beams or the beam angles of reflectors used in discharge fittings tend to span a range of about 10 to 60 degrees, so how will beam angles "fit" the tree? A narrow beam will obviously suit a columnar European white birch, eucalyptus, or sequoia, while a large willow, with its spreading canopy, may well need more than one wide-beam unit.

**Tree structure**

The next consideration is structure. Will the structure of the tree allow the light to penetrate upwards? An open structure allows light to reach up through the canopy to highlight the trunk and branches. As a rule, if you can stand at the base of the trunk and look up through the canopy to the upper branches, uplighting from the base of the tree will be a successful technique.

Some trees, especially many conifers, will fail this simple test, because the canopy is dense and starts at or near ground level, so uplighting from below will tend to produce a green glow that fades out long before the light has penetrated the upper reaches. For such trees, the usual treatment is "washing" the exterior of the tree with light, although you may also be able to shoot a narrow beam up close to the trunk to add a little drama.

At the same time as assessing the openness of the tree structure to determine the feasibility of lighting it, think about the desirability of doing so. Winter, of course, will reveal the structure of a deciduous tree starkly and dramatically under lighting. The beauty of a tree with an inherently pleasing branching structure can be most effectively displayed during dormancy, but a tree with tangled or wind-damaged branches will be revealed for the eyesore that it is. In autumn and winter find other subjects in the garden to light, or light the tree selectively.

**Lighting within the canopy**

Uplighting will produce markedly

different effects according to the position of the fixture or fixtures in relation to the tree and the choice of bulbs. Depending on the shape and size of the tree, decide if certain features need emphasis and consider how lighting inside or outside the canopy can best achieve this. When we uplight a tree from underneath, we are lighting it from inside the canopy. If only one fixture is being used, it should be placed sufficiently close to the base of the tree to light the trunk from near the ground, but not halfway up, otherwise the tree will look as though it is floating. The bulb chosen should have a sufficiently wide beam to light a good portion of the canopy. Placing the light close to the trunk will emphasize the texture and color of the bark, while uplighting from below will emphasize the graceful structure of an open branching tree. Lighting the canopy from within also reveals it against the silhouette of the unlit outer canopy, which provides fascinating depth. Avoid positioning the fixture in a lawn as mowing will be difficult.

**above:** Uplighting in the dense foliage of a chestnut tree fades progressively through the canopy. It becomes more visible as the night sky behind it darkens.

above: The weeping branches of the willow tree sway across the uplighting beam while moon lighting illuminates the euonymus below.

below: The feathery foliage of tree ferns produces one of the most delicate and graceful lighting scenes in the garden.

## Lighting outside the canopy

For larger trees, a combination of two or more fixtures will be required: a narrower beam to light the trunk from near the base, and one or more wider beam units further out to light the canopy. Whether the canopy lighting uplights are placed inside or outside the canopy may depend on several factors, but principally the density of the canopy. In the case of open structure and canopy, lighting from underneath preserves the depth of internal illumination. For trees with a dense canopy positioning fixtures to light from outside is the only option. If possible retain a central narrow beam unit to shoot a beam of light up the trunk. Although many columnar and pyramidal trees can be lit only from outside the canopy, the position of the fixture will determine whether shape or texture is emphasized. Placing the fixture so that it lights up the outside of the tree from within an aiming angle of 15 degrees from the vertical will produce a grazing effect and will emphasize texture. This is within the range of internal adjustment available in many recessed uplights. Siting the fixture further away, with an aiming angle of up to 40 degrees from the vertical, will provide a more uniform wash of light that will show more of the shape of the tree. This degree of adjustment will require spike-mounted spotlights in adjacent planting areas or adjustable surface-mounted fixtures fixed to low walls or structures. Paving, roots, lawn, tree seats, and swings below the tree may get in the way of your ideal choice of position and type of fixture, so some compromises may be required.

## Smaller trees

For many trees up to about 33 feet high, low-voltage halogen uplights of 50–100 watts, used singly or in twos or threes, will produce a stunning effect at reasonable cost. To uplight small trees use one or more spike-mounted spotlights or recessed uplights with a minimum bulb wattage of 50 watts and

a beam angle to suit the tree. An angle of 24 degrees would suit a slender European white birch; 60 degrees would be appropriate for a weeping tree or spreading canopy; and 36–40 degrees would suit most tree shapes that fall in between.

Smaller specimens in walled gardens and courtyards may also be lit. Lighting a wall or hedge to silhouette a small tree in front is an interesting effect if the tree has an open structure. Alternatively, a spotlight in front can project the shadow of a tree onto the wall behind. This is a good way of using, for example, a small maple to create a big effect in a newly planted garden. It may be possible to vary the effect from season to season. You could uplight a maple during the summer that is shadowed or silhouetted in winter (see pages 47 and 52) by moving the low-voltage spotlight forward relative to the subject or behind it to graze a wall against which the tree will be seen in dark outline. To uplight the trunk, locate the fitting about 20 inches from the trunk for a 50-watt wide-beam bulb and up to 3 feet for a 100-watt unit.

### Larger trees

For darker, denser, or larger specimens, higher-power, low-voltage uplights are available in both recessed and surface-mount types and use 75-watt dichroic or 75- or 100-watt metal-reflector halogen

bulbs. The largest trees may require more than the focused power of several 75- or 100-watt halogen reflector bulbs, so light sources other than halogen may have to be considered. This is because the higher-power linear halogen bulb used in floodlights is fine for applications in security lighting but is not well suited to lighting up into a tree without blasting wasted light into the night sky. So the choice lies between higher-power halogen spotlights and discharge bulbs designed for focused lighting applications.

Halogen sources such as 300-watt PAR56 projector bulbs have been widely used in the past, and their slightly yellow light can provide a warm feel to rich brown bark. On the other hand, halogen lighting tends to give foliage a brownish tinge. It is also relatively energy inefficient and produces considerable heat, which means that it may need to be shielded to protect people from accidental contact, or require guards, which can restrict light output or accumulate litter. Of the discharge light sources, sodium lighting addresses the energy efficiency issue, but its yellow light and poor color rendering make it a poor choice for lighting trees.

On the other hand, single-ended metal halide bulbs are ideal for focused lighting applications, are energy efficient and cooler running, and are available in different "color temperatures" so the color can be matched to the needs of

**far left:** Uplighting the trunk emphasizes bark texture often missed in daylight. The proximity of paths, a pool area, and nearby houses preclude lighting of the canopy from the outside, leaving an inner glow against the night sky as the legacy of lighting from below.

**above left:** The reflective white bark and silver underside of the foliage of a European white birch make them beautiful lighting subjects with only low-power bulbs.

the subject. The lowest color temperature, 3000K (see page 16), provides the same, slightly golden-white light as halogen bulbs and tends to flatter the mid-green foliage of broadleaf trees, the lighter foliage of robinias and acacias, the silvery undersides of some foliage, and the white and colored bark of many ornamental species. However, using this warm color to uplight trees with a blue or gray tinge to the foliage, such as some pines and cedars, tends to make them look rather gray and dusty. A simple change to a bulb with a

**above:** Metal halide bulbs with a 4000K blue tinged color temperature emphasize the foliage color of this cedar of Lebanon.

## UPLIGHTING TREES: BULB POWER AND BEAM ANGLE

The illustrations below show the approximate height of trees (in feet) that can be lit by the principal combinations of bulb wattage and beam angle.

### metal halide

| | | | | | |
|---|---|---|---|---|---|
| 10° 35 watts 65 ft. | 30° 35 watts 40 ft. | 50° 35 watts 30 ft. |
| 10° 70 watts 80 ft. | 30° 70 watts 50 ft. | 50° 70 watts 40 ft. |
| 10° 150 watts 100 ft. | 30° 150 watts 80 ft. | 50° 150 watts 50 ft. |

### tungsten halogen

| | | | |
|---|---|---|---|
| 12° 75 watts 50 ft. | 24° 75 watts 30 ft. | 36° 75 watts 20 ft. | 60° 75 watts 15 ft. |
| | 24° 100 watts 50 ft. | 36° 100 watts 25 ft. | |

slightly bluer, cooler color rendering of, say, 4200K, will bring such a tree to life.

Conversely, if you have used a cooler bulb—that is one with a higher color temperature—to uplight an oak or beech tree, the bluish tinge to the light will give the tree a ghostly feel, which can be simply corrected by changing to a warmer bulb. Metal halide fixtures rely on internal reflectors for beam control, but the fact that a metal halide bulb is physically larger than a halogen capsule means that the optical control is less refined. This has the advantage of producing a controlled central beam that can be used for lighting the trunk and branch structure, and a peripheral spread to light the canopy. The uplight can, therefore, be placed farther from the trunk, making it easier to avoid the tree's roots.

Lighting large trees requires powerful fixtures that are normally associated with commercial projects, but the powerful lighting must be contained within the garden boundaries so that light does not trespass into neighboring windows. You may also want to light the trees from one side only—you might, for instance, want to see the tree from the house but not have it appear too boldly to the outside world. Environmentally conscious homeowners might wish to avoid overuse of electricity.

### Plants

Tastes in garden lighting vary widely, and nowhere is this more so than in the treatment of planting. Some people prefer to light only subjects that can be classified as focal points and will include planting only if it is distinctly architectural

---

**LIGHTING TOPIARY**

Lighting architectural planting for its inherent features is one thing, but lighting topiary is completely different. It is more akin to lighting statues and focal points, and indeed that is often its role, especially in formal layouts or small gardens. Grazing up trimmed cones of box or bay can work well to emphasize texture. A second fixture can be used to establish the shape against the darkness. Other subjects need either more space to allow for crosslighting of complex manicured shapes, or additional lighting angles to show shape fully. Mophead trees tend to look like green wine glasses if they are only uplit from underneath, because there is a shadow on the top half of the sphere. To see the full shape, you would need to add either downlighting from a structure or crosslighting at the height of the standards.

or size to the garden. People are more comfortable when they are able to see the extent of their surroundings, and lighting the planting can achieve this. Even so, being selective will pay off; light good specimens and aim for contrast. Where the border offers rich contrast and a wealth of differing specimen planting, then night lighting will paint a colorful tapestry.

### Leaf and flower color

Color is an important factor in the lighting of shrub borders. Darker-leaved specimens are less reflective than lighter-colored or variegated foliage. Lighting camellias and rhododendrons in flower can be stunning, but for the rest of the year their dark, opaque leaves are fairly boring subjects for illumination unless companion planting offers seasonal alternatives. Pale lime-green or silvery foliage stands out well under relatively low levels of lighting, while variegation adds contrast to individual plants to capture attention. Individual specimens, such as those listed on pages 80–81, may impart particularly colorful leaves, stems, flowers, or berries. Flowers in pale colors, such as pink, yellow, and particularly white, stand out readily under relatively low levels of light—for example, white roses climbing over an arc—can be eye-catching with a little uplighting.

in character. For other people, garden lighting is all about an illuminated horticultural panorama, in which focal points other than plants are irrelevant.

Infill lighting in shrub borders is often used to link illuminated focal points so that the eye can pan comfortably across the complete scene without having to adapt repeatedly to light and dark. It is also important to light enough of the whole garden to give some impression of shape and space. Lighting odd objects dotted across the landscape gives them neither a sense of place nor brings any sense of unity

## Plant texture and shape

Texture is another oft-forgotten characteristic. It may be the texture of the plant's own leaves and stems that is highlighted by lighting, but more often it will be the overall impression of a group of plants. A screen of bamboo, for example, makes an interesting textural wall if it is grazed diagonally across the surface to bring out the pattern of its foliage, rather than uplighting to emphasize its stature. Plants with strong leaf shapes offer opportunities for projecting shadows up through the plant or onto adjacent surfaces, and architectural plants can make striking features.

## Uplighting and crosslighting

Uplighting tends to be the main technique used because overhead lighting positions are rare in most gardens. Spike-mounted spotlights are generally preferable, as they are less likely to be covered by lower level or ground-cover planting at the front of the border than recessed uplights. There are exceptions, however. Recessed uplights are better for uplighting specimen plants in open gravel areas, for example, they may also be more resistant to damage by pets. Spike-mounted spotlights are more flexible in crosslighting shrub borders than frontal uplighting, because angling the fixture to provide an oval beam spread along the border can increase the area of coverage, as well as increasing the contrast between light and shadow.

In winter, variegated evergreens, colorful stems, berries, dried stems, foliage, and seed heads provide a strong impact under lighting. In summer, lighting in borders often appears less bright than in winter, as the light is absorbed by darker, denser foliage. This is when the flexibility of low-voltage systems comes into play: bulbs can be repositioned and refocused according to which specimens are of current interest. Spike-mounted uplights can be more easily maneuvered in this context.

## Downlighting and moon lighting

Where planting is dense, downlighting

from trees and taller structures can introduce wide coverage and provide a contrast for uplighting. This is particularly important if flowers rather than foliage are the key to the garden design. Flowers tend to face upward and are not seen at their best when they are lit from below, and uplighting is often masked by lower foliage. Downlighting from a pergola beam, post, or wall is an effective way of highlighting the flowers of climbing plants as well as of providing overlapping lighting onto a path or patio beneath. Moon lighting down from a tree is a subtle way of lighting grass areas planted with bulbs or to light herbaceous borders where planting density conspires against uplighting of individual plants.

**above left:** The white panicles of pampas grass catch the light, while the slender outward-curving leaves add structure to the view.

---

### WHITE LIGHT

The white light typical of halogen bulbs and some discharge light sources flatter the natural colors of flowers and foliage to achieve a more natural-looking color. Using a green spotlight to light a specimen plant is more likely to make it look like an artificial Christmas tree. The best choice for uplighting darker, larger shrubs in a mature garden is often a 50-watt, 36–60-degree bulb. In smaller gardens, with less mature planting or with particularly light-colored subjects, 35-watt bulbs with 36–60-degree beams will provide adequate effect. In roof gardens and small courtyards, use 20 watts to avoid overlighting in a small space; this also reduces the risk of glare from overly bright bulbs.

| SPECIMEN PLANTS | |
| --- | --- |
| **PLANT** | **CHARACTERISTICS AS A GOOD LIGHTING SUBJECT** |
| *Acanthus mollis*<br>Bear's breeches | Large, shiny leaves and extraordinary spikes of white flowers |
| *Acer palmatum* **var.** *dissectum*<br>Japanese maple | Arching branches of deeply dissected leaves provide texture and autumn color |
| *Aralia elata* 'Variegata'<br>Japanese angelica tree | Spreading branches of large, elegant leaves with creamy white borders |
| *Buddleja davidii* 'Harlequin'<br>Butterfly bush | Arching branches of variegated gray-green and white leaves and deep purple flowers |
| *Buxus sempervirens*<br>Common boxwood | Ideal plant for clipping into a topiary shapes to be lit as statuary |
| *Cimicifuga simplex* 'Brunette'<br>Autumn snakeroot | Dark, brownish-purple shiny leaves and tall stems of white flowers in autumn |
| *Cordyline australis* 'Sundance'<br>New Zealand cabbage palm | Large, arching, lance-shaped leaves |
| *Cornus alba* 'Elegantissimma'<br>Redtwig dogwood | Upright scarlet red stems |
| *Cortaderia selloana* 'Sunningdale Silver'<br>Pampas grass | Tall mound of arching leaves and upright plumes of silvery flowers |
| *Corylus avellana* 'Contorta'<br>Corkscrew hazel | Corkscrew-like branches and yellow catkins |
| *Cotinus coggygria* 'Royal Purple'<br>Purple smoke bush | Almost translucent, reddish-purple leaves, which turn scarlet in autumn |
| *Cynara cardunculus*<br>Cardoon | Large, dissected, silvery-gray leaves and thick stems of large, purple, thistle-like flowers |
| *Dicksonia antarctica*<br>Man fern | Wonderful subject for lighting; hairy trunk and large, arching, fern-like leaves |
| *Digitalis purpurea* f. *albiflora*<br>White foxglove | Tall stems of pendulous white bells arise from basal rosettes of large furry leaves |
| *Dryopteris filix-mas*<br>Male fern | Large, arching fronds |
| *Eryngium pandanifolium*<br>Sea holly | Silvery-green, sword-like leaves |
| *Exochorda* x *macrantha* 'The Bride'<br>*Pearlbush* | Arching branches adorned with hanging bunches of white flowers in late spring |
| *Fatsia japonica* 'Variegata'<br>Japanese fatsia | Architectural evergreen shrub with large, glossy green and white leaves |
| *Gunnera manicata*<br>Giant rhubarb | Prickly stalks holding aloft almost the largest leaves of any temperate plant |

| SPECIMEN PLANTS | |
|---|---|
| **PLANT** | **CHARACTERISTICS AS A GOOD LIGHTING SUBJECT** |
| *Hosta sieboldiana* var. *elegans*<br>Plantain lily | Large, ribbed, blue-green leaves with pale lilac-gray flowers |
| *Matteuccia struthiopteris*<br>Ostrich fern | Lime-green, translucent upright fronds |
| *Melianthus major*<br>Honey bush | Large, evergreen, serrated blue-green leaves |
| *Miscanthus sinensis*<br>Eulalia grass | Tall grass with long, arching leaves |
| *Onopordum acanthium*<br>Cotton thistle | Gray spiny leaves and round, purple, thistle-like flowers |
| *Phormium tenax* 'Sundowner'<br>New Zealand flax | Fans of tall linear leaves striped dark green and pink |
| *Phyllostachys nigra*<br>Black bamboo | Tall upright stems mature to a dark brown or black; dramatic plant for lighting |
| *Prunus laurocerasus* 'Otto Luyken'<br>Cherry laurel | Cultivar with large, shiny, evergreen leaves and clusters of white flowers in spring |
| *Prunus lusitanica*<br>Portugal laurel | Red stems and dark evergreen leaves; the cultivar *P. l.* 'Variegata' has green and white leaves and is even more effective |
| *Rheum palmatum*<br>Chinese rhubarb | Very large, coarsely toothed leaves which are green above and purple-red beneath |
| *Rhus typhina* 'Dissecta'<br>Staghorn sumac | Gently contorted stems that bear dissected leaves which turn brilliant scarlet in autumn |
| *Rosa moyesii*<br>Rose | Arching stems of pink roses in midsummer, followed by large, flask-shaped, red hips |
| *Rubus biflorus* | Conspicuous white stems in winter |
| *Salix exigua*<br>Coyote willow | Fine silvery foliage—one of the best gray-leaved plants for lighting |
| *Sambucus nigra* f. *laciniata*<br>Black elder | A lovely elder with finely cut, green leaves |
| *Sambucus racemosa* 'Plumosa Aurea'<br>European red elder | Golden, serrated leaves and red berries |
| *Sisyrinchium striatum* 'Aunt May' | Clumps of evergreen, green and cream, iris-like foliage |
| *Verbascum olympicum*<br>Mullein | The tall spikes of gray-white, woolly leaves topped with bright yellow flowers |
| *Viburnum plicatum* 'Mariesii' | Tiered branches with pendulous leaves and erect white flowers |
| *Yucca filamentosa*<br>Adam's needle | Sharply pointed, sword-like, evergreen leaves |

**above:** This brightly lit statue is the center of attention. The exotic planting has been lit less brightly, so as not to detract from it.

**right:** Uplighting this bust of Brutus against the dark niche in the hedge behind illustrates the importance of contrasting light and darkness in emphasizing drama in focal points.

interpreted sensitively and the lighting carefully placed if the subject is to be attractively illuminated. A figure of a woman turning shyly to the left will be emphasized if it is lit mainly from the right, while a boldly striding or running figure must be lit strongly to emphasize the line and outline that convey this movement. The face must be illuminated appropriately, with subtlety for a shy, upward glance and with boldness, possibly including deep shadow, for a strong male figure or animal sculpture, such as a lion. An upward-facing figure seeking inspiration from the sky will not be enhanced by uplighting from below, which will merely emphasize the chin below the unlit face and features. The intensity of light and its direction will intensify movement and expression only if we can appreciate the viewing angle— lighting a face for frontal expression is pointless if the statue is subsequently positioned to gaze in profile toward a further vista.

### Locating statues

The site of the statue will also determine the lighting scheme, both in its brightness relative to other statues

## Statues and focal points

Statues and focal points need to be brightly lit if they are to fulfill their role as centers of attention. If there are several focal points in a view, they need not be illuminated equally—some should be treated as having secondary or tertiary importance and be lit less brightly. A pair of urns flanking a view through to a statue beyond should be lit less brightly than the statue, which is the primary focus. Moreover, because the statue is farther away, it will need to be more brightly lit than the closer urns. For example, if the statue were at the same approximate distance as the urns, lighting the urns with 20-watt bulbs and the statue with a 35-watt bulb would establish the primacy of the statue within the view. If the statue were further away than the urns, trading up to a 50-watt bulb would preserve its dominance.

### Lighting statues

A statue is a very individual statement in a garden. It is a reflection of the owner's personal taste, so its character must be

or focal points and in relation to its surroundings. A classical warrior posed in front of a hedge is like an actor on a stage, so additional lighting behind the statue or to either side to wash the hedge will provide the appropriate theatrical backdrop. This will also help to avoid lumpy shadows being projected onto the hedge. On the other hand, a running figure or animal sculpture may be pictured as running out of a dark void for strong contrast with the darkness behind, which will emphasize drama and movement. A statue may also be tucked away in a corner as a surprise for the evening stroller, and the lighting can reflect its surreptitious or mischievous presence.

Bulky plinths can get in the way of good lighting, but sometimes recessed uplights can be engineered into large plinths, provided that it is considered when the lighting circuits and statue are first planned. Remember to throw a little light onto the plinth itself so that the statue does not appear to be airborne in darkness, unless that is the specific intention, for a subject such as a flying bird or mythological figure.

**above:** The Buddha at the top of the water staircase is lit for prominence in the view.

### Other focal points

Other types of focal points share many of the same characteristics as statues when it comes to lighting, whether they are urns, troughs, armillary spheres,

---

### COMPARATIVE POWER OF LIGHTING REQUIRED TO COMPENSATE FOR DISTANCE FROM VIEWPOINT (HALOGEN BULBS)

A statue that is situated at some distance from the viewpoint must be lit more brightly than one that is situated close to the window or patio from which it is mainly observed in order to achieve the same impact.

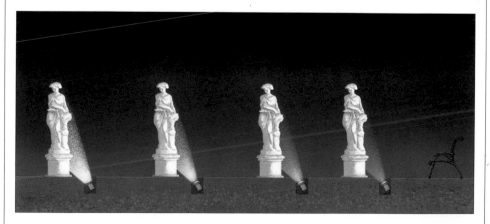

| 50 ft. | 30 ft. | 15 ft. | 7 ft. | **DISTANCE** |
| 75 watts | 50 watts | 35 watts | 20 watts | **BULB POWER** |

**above:** Uplighting would have resulted in a dark equine face above a bright plinth. Moon lighting from a tree provides a dappled, less dramatic lighting effect, which also provides background from the pampas grass.

**below:** The light-colored statue and white tulips are highly reflective with relatively low power lighting. Gentle uplighting and moon lighting of the avenue of apple trees behind adds depth to the view.

sundials, or obelisks. Water features, decorative panels in walls and paving, and some garden structures are, of course, also focal points, and the same rules relating to distance from viewpoint and establishing a hierarchy apply to them. Ornamental benches can be difficult, because lighting them as focal points may result in glare that will be uncomfortable for anyone sitting there. Downlighting from a structure or tree is the best solution if such mounting points are available.

### Color and lighting intensity

The intensity of lighting required depends on color as much as on the distance of the subject from the viewpoint, or its brightness relative to the background and other focal points. The high reflectance of a white marble subject makes a low lighting intensity necessary, otherwise it may be overly lit, producing a bright white glow instead of subtle shadows. On the other hand, dark bronze statues have a very low reflectance and will need fairly bright lighting if they are to stand out as focal points from any distance. The problem with bronze is that it is often shiny, and, if you light it with a few beams of very high-intensity lighting,

you will be rewarded by a high-intensity shine. The trick with bronze statues is to use a larger number of lower-power sources, each directed toward a separate part of the statue selectively, but with sufficient overlap to make the lighting effect look complete. This may involve using narrower-beam spotlights to emphasize facial expression, muscular tone, or particular ornaments, while filling in other parts with a wash of light from wider-beam spotlights.

Other color challenges will present themselves in planning lighting effects. Light statues on dark plinths will stand out well while the plinth remains of secondary importance. In the reverse situation, you may struggle to focus enough light on a dark subject for it to stand out without stray light emphasizing the lightness of the plinth. Sometimes the simplest answer is to encourage the lighter stone plinth to weather so that the balance is correct even in daylight.

### Uplighting statues

Uplighting from directly in front of a statue or focal point can produce a washed-out, two-dimensional effect (especially for a light-colored subject). Close uplighting can project strong

shadows onto the upper part of a figure from protrusions at a lower level. Such shadows give a sense of menace to a face, and occasionally this is useful for exaggerating facial expressions.

If, however, it is a figure with arms akimbo or holding an object below face level, the face may be totally hidden. The answer is to position the fixture back about 20 inches from the base of the statue to give the light beam a chance to light the planes of the face, neck, and shoulders. An uplight placed slightly to one side of the viewing axis will highlight form and relief with contrasting light and subtle shadow for a fuller effect, avoiding the cardboard cutout effect of frontal lighting. Spike-mounted spotlights are easily moved to customize the effect on installation, but recessed uplights may need to be set in concrete niches in paving before the statue reaches the site, so no adjustment is possible apart from that available by tilting the bulb cradle within the recessed body.

### Crosslighting statues

Lighting from one side only can leave a statue looking curiously lopsided, so consider crosslighting from two opposing directions, using lighting of different intensities to achieve crosslit shadow while maintaining all-around illumination. This can be achieved either by changing the bulb on one side to a lower wattage or having a different beam spread to diffuse the light. Alternatively, moving one spotlight 3 feet further away can be enough to make the difference. Spike-mounted spotlights hidden in the edge of planted areas are convenient and flexible, although crosslighting may also be achieved with surface-mounted spotlights mounted on a wall, pergola or tree. Downlighting from these same positions may be the answer for some upward-facing statues, those on large plinths or planted containers, in which the plant might be hidden from uplighting by the lip of the jardiniere. In practice, many features benefit from a combination of uplighting, downlighting, and crosslighting. Sometimes, accent lighting from one source makes a feature stand out, while infill lighting adds a diffuse element to soften hard shadows or a stark scene. While simple one-direction lighting will add drama to a subject, the addition of an extra dimension is worthwhile. For example, a phormium in an attractive urn can be downlit, while a soft uplight will show the form of the container.

**above:** Spotlighting onto the phormium from the house wall highlights the architectural leaf form while casting shadow within the pool of light framing the gravel oval. This is a perfect illustration of fitting the oval pool of light to the shape on the ground.

left: Grazing up the house wall emphasizes the texture, as well as the color of the brickwork, while also silhouetting the magnolia tree. The whole view is reflected in a rectangular pond to be enjoyed from the temple (see page 61).

## Structures

Architectural lighting techniques may also apply to features and backdrops around the garden. Outbuildings designed to relate to the architectural features of the home should be lit to match, whether as an accompaniment to a path, a backdrop to a statue, an invitation to other areas such as a guesthouse or pool area, or as features in their own right.

### Follies

Some buildings may merely be follies built as focal points rather than functional structures, while decorative facades or false doorways can ornament purely functional buildings. Many ideas fundamental to architectural lighting are described on pages 41–44; it just needs a little imagination to recognize features of architectural merit and to apply appropriate techniques. Of course, freestanding arches and other structures built as perspective and decorative devices are also an invitation to experiment with lighting skills. An arch, for example, may be used to divide two areas. Consider uplighting to draw attention to it as the threshold to another outdoor room or to frame the view through it to a focal point.

### Gazebos

Gazebos are built to provide a viewpoint over the garden as a whole or a particular scene or feature. Bear this in mind before lighting such features purely as focal points in their own right, because ornamental lighting of the structure must be carefully placed to avoid glare to people wandering in and taking a seat. Gentle uplighting or moon lighting is better than crosslighting, which is likely to be invasive within the structure.

Interior downlighting will avoid an "unoccupied" feel and can be used to illuminate decorative floor detail, but remember that less is more, and keep it soft. The difference between lighting for mood and lighting for reading can be important in these structures. It is essential to decide priorities at the outset. Downlighting in a gazebo that is bright enough to facilitate reading will not encourage anyone to sit there quietly to look out on ornamentally lit features. Options for alternative levels of lighting, including the ability to switch off interior downlighting, should be provided.

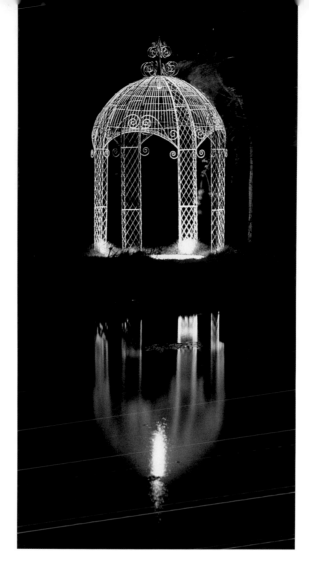

**above:** Four 20-watt uplights make this Victorian cablework gazebo stand out in the darkness and allow reflection in the water in the foreground. A small white 20-watt downlight at the apex illuminates mosaic tiling below.

---

## ARCHITECTURAL LIGHTING

**ILLUMINATION CAN BE USED TO EMPHASIZE THE STRUCTURE AND DETAILS OF BUILDINGS IN THE GARDEN. SIMPLE IDEAS ARE OFTEN THE MOST EFFECTIVE.**

- Recess downlights under a porch canopy to illuminate the front door and provide a focus for visitors.
- Uplight buttresses or columns with narrow beams to emphasize their structure.
- Introduce uplights between windows, using narrow- or medium-beam bulbs, to illuminate the facade without causing glare indoors.
- Uplight architectural planting to throw the shadows of branches and leaves onto blank walls.
- Wash lighting down facades over porches or lower structures to reveal their shape distinctly from the main building.
- Crosslight steps leading up to doors for safety and to emphasize the texture of the paving.
- Use narrow-beam spotlights to emphasize unusual wall features, such as plaques, clocks, or relief panels.
- Use shielded fixtures to light window reveals and to emphasize interesting arches or cornices.
- Use interior lighting to emphasize unusual glazed features, such as stained glass or unusually shaped windows.
- Graze up brick or stone walls from near the base to emphasize their texture and color.

**above:** Uplighting the pergola columns also illuminates the wide-spreading branches of the tree and is complemented by downlighting from between the beams.

## Pergolas

Pergolas can be illuminated by uplighting the climbing plants that are scrambling up the supporting piers, or by downlighting with fixtures on the cross beams or the top of the posts or columns. A combination of the two approaches is often the best choice, but will depend on the function of the pergola. If it is primarily an ornamental feature or serves the function of an archway framing a view, uplighting will emphasize the structure and the material of which the uprights are built, as well as casting light across plants creeping along the cross beams.

The power of the lighting required will be determined at least partly by the color of the material, whether the evening sky or a dark area is behind it, and by its distance from the focal point. Narrow-beam 20- or 35-watt bulbs in spike-mounted or recessed uplights will generally be the right choice. It is usually a good idea to incorporate some element of gentle downlighting to bring the ground into the picture. Pergolas are often built as places to sit and possibly to dine, with associated focal points nearby. Such focal points then become the prime view and the pergola provides the ambience around and over the seating, while downlights mounted on the pergola or among adjacent planting illuminate the focal point.

## Walkways

Where there is a seating area beneath a pergola or a path through it, you may want to consider downlighting as the dominant technique. For a walkway through a pergola, downlighting at the top of columns can show upward-facing

**right:** 20-watt downlights in the top of the lattice columns provide a network of patterned light and shadow along the path. Spotlighting the statue at the end provides a focal point for strollers and from the terrace from which the path leads.

**below:** Small area lighting fixtures, featuring 20-watt, halogen capsule bulbs, are mounted on each upright to provide general lighting for sitting out and also an attractive wash of light which brings out the color of the terra-cotta wall.

flowers as well as casting the shadow of the climbing plants down onto the path. This can leave the cross beams unlit. This may not be important if they are silhouetted against glow from city lights, if there are no climbing plants growing across them, or if there is a focal point at the end of a pergola that is framed by the illuminated columns advancing toward it. Often, however, the best solution will be a combination of uplighting on the columns and downlighting from the cross beams to provide path lighting beneath.

### Dining areas

Where the pergola frames a dining area, downlighting can illuminate the table while uplighting casts light on the surrounding "room" created by the shrub borders or climbing plants growing up the supporting columns or posts. If the pergola is small and huddles closely around the dining table, uplighting the nearby columns or posts will cause glare for anyone who happens to glance backward. In a closely confined area, it is preferable to use mainly downlighting with fixtures fitted with internal glare louvres or external glare guards, both over the table and

**above:** Uplighting from the planters projects shadows onto the walls while downlights provide illumination over the seating area. Sails and canopies can be used to diffuse and reflect light.

**right:** Ornamental lighting provides the ambience of this outdoor room. Candles on the table provide a mellow contrast to electric lighting.

down the adjacent posts to light the surroundings of the posts and dining chairs. If the pergola has a large tree nearby, moon lighting down can add a romantic touch with its subtle effect, throwing gentle light and the shadow of beams and climbers onto the table below. Even then, do not forget to put candles on the table for a final touch of intimacy. Remember that if directional lighting is used close to areas that people use, fixtures with glare-control features must be used. The lighting must be soft enough to create a pleasant ambience, and fixtures must be carefully positioned both to avoid glare and to ensure that faces are not left in shadow. Bulbs should be 20 watts, at most 35 watts, with wide beams.

### Area lighting

Area lighting products are sometimes used for illuminating pergola areas, and although some small fixtures make an unobtrusive contribution toward the ambience of a dining area under a pergola, larger ones can be overly bright and draw the eye away from the scene. Halogen capsule bulbs can be contained within small fixtures located between the beams or color-matched to the posts or columns to be unobtrusive.

Hanging lanterns are often a hazard to taller visitors. Fixtures designed for the walls of the house should not clutter a decorative structure or provide obstacles at head height to bump into. Using such unsuitable lighting products in such contexts looks wrong unless the fittings match a design theme, such as Japanese brass lanterns in a pergola or gazebo designed for an Eastern effect. You must think ahead if you wish to avoid a clutter of visible cabling running up a stone column or brick pier. A conduit within the structure provides cable-ways from the ground up to the pergola beams and is an unobtrusive way of achieving this. Metal structures often feature hollow tubing through which cabling can be threaded. Cable channels can be routed in timber posts so that cabling can be hidden under matching trim pieces prepared at the same time as the posts.

## Steps

Lighting steps for safety is an obvious requirement in a garden, but it can also be decorative. Using downlighting from adjacent lighting platforms is often the best way; downlighting from an adjacent wall can produce step and path lighting accompanied by grazing of attractive brickwork, while moon lighting from a tree can give a natural effect in a country garden. One of the newer techniques is based on the linear lighting techniques described earlier. It consists of running a linear lighting source in a channel under the nosing of the step or fixing a molding or metal extrusion that provides the fixing for the light source as well as shielding it from view as you ascend the steps. It is a stylish approach, but it tends to produce a fairly bright effect because such products are generally developed for commercial and public premises. It is also moderately expensive for domestic use.

**left:** Recessed brick lights illuminate the path while stem-mounted fixtures light the steps upwards. Some uplighting of small trees adds interest.

**right:** Linear lighting in an aluminum extrusion under the nosing of the steps provides bright and distinctive staircase lighting.

### Step lights

If overhead lighting cannot be installed and linear lighting would be too expensive, crosslighting the steps from the flanking walls is one of the best techniques for lighting steps. Recessed step lights, normally using 20-watt dichroic reflector bulbs to project beams across a staircase, graze across the treads to display texture and color, and to light them for access.

Step lighting should be as uniform as possible, lighting both risers and treads to avoid shadowing from one step onto the next. On an extended staircase, there should be no glare directed downward into the eyes of the ascending pedestrian. The key to fulfilling these requirements without using blander area lighting techniques is to use more fixtures, each one lighting across two, or at most three, steps. Using wider-beam, higher-brightness bulbs may keep the cost down, but it will provide poor uniformity, with dangerous shadow and increased glare. Wider staircases may be lit by using narrower-beam bulbs to project further across the steps, but be careful to guard against glare.

Most step lights are essentially recessed spotlights. You may need to use internal glare louvres or products

---

## LINEAR LIGHTING FOR STEPS

The aluminum extrusion is fixed under the stair nosing. A linear "light string" fitted with long-life bulbs is installed in the channel, cabled to a remote low-voltage transformer and covered with a protective, clear, polycarbonate cover.

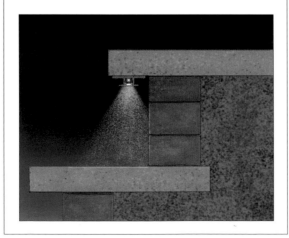

with shielding grilles or eyelid hoods. Make sure that any step light facing a terrace, path, window, or other viewpoint is of a low-glare type, using a capsule bulb rather than a spotlight-type bulb. Such products are sometimes designed for surface-mounting and are fairly small because they contain only a small capsule bulb and do not have to cater for a larger reflector bulb. These can be installed where it is not possible or desirable to bore holes in the walls. Another option is a brick light flushed into the wall. These area lighting products provide a subtle light and will avoid the directional glare of a spotlight. A brick light with an opal lens but without a louvred front may still appear as a bit of a "hot spot" while louvres to prevent glare will cut out half of the light and limit spread to a smaller semicircle, which, in turn, requires more fixtures.

### Spread lights for steps

Where there is no flanking wall, it is best to diffuse light from the side. Some surface-mounted step lights are available on spike-mounting stems so that they can be tucked into hedges and adjacent planting to provide a small pool of light for two or three narrow steps. For wider steps, a wider pool of light is required, but it is a good idea to have a hood over the light source to conceal the bulb. This is how the spread light, or "mushroom light" as many consumers think of it, was born. Selecting a spread light that will stand up high enough to perform its lighting job yet still be visually acceptable is the necessary trade-off. Typical spread lights use a halogen bulb of about 20 watts and provide a circle of coverage of 6–8 feet in diameter for a 1-foot-tall light, increasing to a 11–13 foot diameter for one that is 2 feet tall.

### Paths

The same considerations and design techniques discussed for steps (see pages 91–92) also apply to paths, although the length of the path is likely to be greater than the width of the steps, so the emphasis is on the spread of light. This means that brick lights and spread lights will be the preferred fittings, although downlighting and moon lighting will be the preferred decorative techniques. Where the path is wide or the circulation area is a larger one, area lighting techniques, as applied in some cases to driveways, may come into play.

The fundamental difference between lighting a level route and lighting changes of level: people are

**below:** Step lights hidden under treads light some steps directly and others by reflecting the light around the area from surrounding walls.

**above:** A downlight on the arch and spreadlights in adjacent borders provide effective path lighting. Uplighting of planting provides a sense of space and security along the route.

see regular lighting patterns, but in an informal setting, too much regularity can destroy the atmosphere. As long as there is enough lighting to enable a person to walk along the path without having to think too consciously about it, they can also enjoy illuminated features along the way. It does not matter if the layout is not strictly spaced or if fixtures are paired along either side of the path or staggered on either side. As long as the pools of light from the various sources overlap, or nearly so, then it will be uniform enough.

**Driveways**

Lighting driveways is usually a compromise between providing good lighting and keeping the light sources invisible, but this is not always possible. Moon lighting from trees is an attractive way of lighting a horizontal surface in a natural way that is suitable for both town and country gardens. However, if there are no trees, walls, or structures to act as lighting platforms, the light fittings are bound to be visible. Area lighting on walls or lanterns perched on gate pillars will provide lighting that is mainly for orientation purposes—that is, giving enough light to see by, to find the way, to fetch and carry objects, and to perform simple tasks, such as finding a key.

accustomed to walking along a level surface and need less lighting than for negotiating steps, unless there are obstacles, such as children's toys, lying around. Lighting focal points and adjacent planting for a reassuring ambience also serves to waymark the route, so in most gardens path lighting does not need to be as bright or uniform as step lighting. Indeed, it can be a useful means of avoiding the "runway" effect of regularly spaced fixtures along a straight path.

Regular spacing of lighting helps to make sure that the eye does not have to try to adapt too frequently to different lighting intensities, which can cause disorientation. However, a path in a garden is usually a meandering, pedestrian route that is intended to allow friends and family to move around a garden while they enjoy each other's company and the garden features. In a formal garden layout we would expect to

Lighting planting and features adjacent to the driveway certainly marks the route, but some lighting will usually be needed for pedestrians to use the road. Around driveways, as well as wide paths and open access areas for parking, bollard lights, which project more outward light than spread lights, will give broader coverage but there will be some increased visibility of the light sources. Small halogen bollards are often popular because of their size, and some models are available in modern shapes and fashionable finishes such as copper and stainless steel. For practical purposes around a driveway, particularly around parking or turning areas, taller line-voltage bollard lights with higher power light sources are required. Column-mounted lanterns—either real or scaled-down streetlights—will always be a popular choice with traditionalists or for lighting on a grand scale, but they are used as daytime ornaments as much as working nighttime light sources.

### Patios and terraces

There is a large number of possible lighting combinations, but for large patio areas, different combinations of wall fixtures and low-power floodlights under the eaves will be required for different functions. Brighter lighting may be necessary when you have to keep an eye on children, whereas something a little less bright would be appropriate for gatherings of adults. Provided this is done with taste and restraint, it can create a satisfactory compromise between mood lighting and the higher light levels needed for activity and security. For smaller, more intimate areas, a more subtle approach is needed. Moon lighting is again the most suitable lighting technique for horizontal areas and atmospheric spaces, but there is not always a large enough tree close by to provide the necessary support.

### Downlighting

Downlighting from below the eaves of a house can be an effective way of lighting paths, terraces, and planting around the house to create a welcoming atmosphere. It can also produce a grazing effect if the lighting of a surface from an oblique angle emphasizes texture, such as roughness in brick or stone and the patterns of the mortar joints. This effect can also be produced by placing uplights close to the base of a wall to create a feeling of warmth and intimacy around a terrace.

Downlights and wall-mounted spotlights should be discreet and match the mounting surface or other external fittings as closely as possible. Glare guards or internal honeycomb louvres are often useful for a soft lighting effect and limiting glare. Recessing weatherproof downlights into the soffit below the eaves can be especially neat. Where structures exist over or next to the area where you require lighting, use ideas for lighting pergola areas (see pages 88–91). Lighting patios often requires a combination of downlights and products that will provide softer area

**below:** Downlights mounted under the eaves above the door make focal points of the urn, viewed from the inside of the house and also the entrance when viewed from the outside.

lighting, and uplights to add contrast and emphasis, by uplighting individual features as well as balustrades, trellises, or walls.

### Area lighting

Wall-mounted lights on the house provide light for a patio area immediately outside French windows or a kitchen door and are the most familiar form of exterior lighting. They generally do a good job in providing the lighting needed for orientation and the performance of general tasks. Fixtures mounted at or just above head height provide lighting for everything below eye level and may cast some decorative light on the wall on which they are mounted, as well as any adjacent planting. At night the lights will draw as much attention to themselves as they do to the area they are intended to light, and for this reason it is important that the style should suit the house and that the bulbs that are fitted are not of excessively high wattage. A wider area of illumination is worthless if it is at the cost of being made to feel uncomfortable because of the glare.

While such lighting is not directional like a spotlight beam, the light produced still has a direction of travel and will produce shadows. Anyone seated with their back to the wall light will see the faces of people seated opposite, but their own faces will be in shadow unless additional lighting has been provided from another direction. Good patio illumination, for dining especially, should be all-enveloping while preserving the view of the illuminated garden or landscape view. It should be cabled by means of a separate switch so that the view out from the house is not inhibited by bright area lighting just outside the windows.

### Barbecues

If you are going to dine outside, the chances are that you may also be cooking there. As with a dinner party indoors, you will want to leave the preparation and cooking areas out of sight once the meal is served. This is a simple matter of having one or more lights near the barbecue that can be switched off separately from the ornamental lighting and the lighting over or around the exterior dining table. The switch for the barbecue lighting should preferably be a weatherproof one near the barbecue.

| ILLUMINATING A BARBECUE | |
|---|---|
| **TYPE OF BARBECUE** | **SUITABLE LIGHTING** |
| **Freestanding barbecue against a wall** | Spotlighting down onto the barbecue or area lighting fixed to wall above |
| **Freestanding barbecue under a pergola** | Spotlights fixed to overhead beams |
| **Freestanding barbecue near a tree** | Spotlight fixed to tree by means of mounting bracket |
| **Freestanding barbecue in open area** | Post-mounted lantern or portable light on nearby table |
| **Barbecue with brick or stone surround** | Post-mounted accent light or spread light on surface mount |
| **Barbecue with raised brick or stone surround** | Brick lights or step lights set into walls at either side |

### Courtyards

In a small space around a dining area, consider gentle uplighting to reveal the shape of the space and the presence of planting to create an intimate feeling that contrasts with the indoor ambience. Uplighting can also throw the shadow of climbing plants upwards onto a rendered wall for added interest. This is particularly appropriate for courtyards, which are often shady places during the day but have walls that offer opportunities for creating a subtle and romantic ambience in the evening. Walls with interesting stone or brickwork can be grazed by uplights or downlights to emphasize the texture, the color of the material, and the shape of the walled enclosure. Low-power downlighting can throw the foliage shadow onto the paving below in an imaginative miniaturization of the moon lighting effect seen with trees.

### Balconies and roof terraces

Lofty terraces on the top or side of buildings have a magic of their own at night: their dizzy height commands a view and it is the job of lighting to reinforce this, not negate it by lighting the space only for its own sake. Lighting should be secondary to the view and consist mainly of low-level lighting across the decking or paving, accepting the wash of interior lighting through picture windows and so easing the transition from interior to exterior. Overhead lighting, if suitable mounting points exist, can perform two functions. First, it should add downlighting for key plants or features; and second, it should provide lighting for dining or reading. Both types of lighting should be cabled on separate switches so that brighter lighting can be switched off to allow the vista beyond to be seen more clearly. Any ornamental lighting, whether it is downlighting or uplighting, must be discreet and concentrate merely on framing the view and contributing a pleasant ambience.

**above left:** The arched trellis feature is lit so that it can be seen through the arch from the seating area in the foreground. The priority is to draw the eye down into the roof garden and away from the surrounding buildings.

# Lighting design
# for the outdoor room

**above:** The uplighting of the bamboo, shrubs, and rock water feature frames the decking and seating area. Spotlights under the plank bridge light the cobblestone streambed.

In an integrated garden design, remembering what not to light and by how much is as important as remembering what to light; a good design will exploit the potential of shadow to create depth and perspective. Although every garden is different, some general guidelines can be applied to creating lighting plans, which can be adapted to suit different types of gardens. The ideas and examples will help you devise a plan for your own garden.

## Editing the view

If you do not light it, you will not see it. Observing this rule for compost heaps, outbuildings, and utility areas may seem obvious and, although lighting for access to these areas may be required for functional reasons, the lights should be on separate circuits so that they can be switched on separately from the ornamental garden lighting. It is also important to consider this rule when you are placing fixtures so that they are carefully directed only at the objects you wish to light and not at the children's jungle gym or other background areas that do not contribute to the ornamental view.

In newly planted gardens, the small size of the initial planting is likely to limit the amount of lighting installed in the first year, unless there are attractive walls or a trellis to stand in as lighting subjects while the plants develop. Unless you are installing an entire system in one go, first-year installation may be limited to areas of hard landscaping, focal points, structures, and any existing mature specimen plants. To attempt more can often result in nothing more than a well-lit fence. The scope for adding fixtures as planting matures should have been planned at the beginning. Avoid overlighting by illuminating every shrub and paving stone. As with so many things, less is more.

## Inside looking out

When you have installed garden lighting, a window ceases to be something to be covered with blinds when dusk falls. Instead, it becomes a frame for the picture of the illuminated garden. However, this only works if the balance of interior and exterior lighting is correct. Insufficient outdoor light results in the "black mirror" effect—you see your own reflection and that of the room around you in the dark glass of the window. If the primary objective is to enjoy the view from the house, the exterior lighting must be brighter than the interior lighting so that the "black mirror" will become transparent glass and allow the view to come through. This is also a matter of making sure that the interior lighting is not too bright or, perhaps, that it can be dimmed according to mood so that the garden illumination becomes more visible.

**above:** The wall fountain provides a focal point to look at from inside the house as well as within the courtyard itself.

**above:** Crosslighting the steps from fixtures tucked under the bottom of the hedge also lights the route through to the next "room." The steps lead the eye through to the illuminated planter beyond, while the urns frame the view. Foreground illumination is provided by area lighting on the house walls.

Nowhere is this more important than in a conservatory where almost the whole room can become a black mirror. In a conservatory, "point" sources of light, such as chandeliers, should be avoided because these are reflected brilliantly in every pane of glass. Using discreet downlighting by surface- or track-mounted spotlights or cable-lighting systems onto interior features and seating areas can produce better results. If a chandelier or decorative lantern is used over a dining table it should be connected to a separate switch so that it can be removed from the view when not needed.

## Setting lighting priorities

Lighting selectively should not depend on random choice. It must be based on establishing a sense of priority within the view. Once the viewpoints are established from windows, as well as from the patio and seats around the garden, each view must have a balanced composition. It is essential to decide on the primary focal point within a view (see pages 82–85), because a pair of objects demanding equal attention can confuse the eye. If there are several important features, perhaps a group of figures, for example,

either light them as a group or establish a hierarchy between them so that the primary focal point is most brightly lit, while features of secondary or tertiary importance are less so.

## Make it easy on the eye

Although we praise the notion of contrasting light and shadow, it is important to remember the difference between shadow and darkness. Shadow is created by light, whereas darkness is the result of an absence of light. Leaving some areas in darkness may be a creative decision so that illuminated objects in the foreground stand out, or so that a vista is maintained if there is a view of a city or landscape from a balcony or roof garden. It may be a result of a fall of the ground if there is no backdrop to light behind the statue or tree and we must be content with the sunset sky or the glitter of stars for our background. There is always a danger of being too selective, either because of a conscious decision to light only one or two features or a lack of awareness of the resulting starkness.

Most subjects benefit from being given a sense of place in the garden, especially by having a background of a hedge, wall, or planting illuminated at a lower level. It is important to provide a link between focal points so that the eye is not continually adapting to brightness and darkness as it pans across the scene. Lighting shrub borders is one of the main ways of achieving this in the vertical plane, but if the horizontal plane is also lit it will add the third dimension to the view. Moon lighting onto a lawn or introducing some simple spread lighting of a path are ways of achieving this.

## Emphasizing depth

Ideas for emphasizing depth and providing a link within the view are always worth considering, but they assume an added importance when we consider perspective, which can appear quite different in artificial lighting compared with daylight conditions. Lighting a statue more brightly will make it appear closer to the viewer, but it will recede further into the view if it is less brightly lit.

The choice of lighting brightness depends partly on the relative importance attributed to the features, but also on its distance from the viewpoint. A small statue placed near the edge of the patio close to the house may well be overly lit by anything more powerful than a 20-watt bulb. If the same statue were placed three times as far away, you would almost certainly need to use a 35-watt or even a 50-watt bulb. Bear in mind that a small statue may be too tiny to be seen from the house, in daylight or at night if it is too far away, and it will therefore lose its role as a focal point. Replacing it with a larger subject at the same distance from the house may require two or more bulbs of 50 watts or more. No matter how brightly we light a subject in relation to its distance from the viewpoint, lighting a distant subject should be avoided if it is not to appear to float in blackness. Aim to achieve a blend between a brighter focal point and a less-bright middle ground consisting of a little light cast on the lawn and illumination of shrub borders on either side. Lighting flanking shrub borders will visually "push" the sides of the garden view outward to make the space feel larger and avoid the tunnel vision that is associated with a single illuminated focal point.

## Front gardens

Front gardens are often neglected areas as far as ornamental lighting is concerned. While paths, steps, and drives usually receive lighting treatment of some kind and lighting around the front door is almost universal,

**below:** Uplighting of the tree and formal features provides an attractive front garden scene when the visitor ascends the illuminated steps.

decorating our home does not often extend to having a front-garden lighting scheme. Lighting decorative features helps to put the home in the context of its plot and to put the paths and steps in the context of the space they cross. Lighting may need to be protected from vandals by being recessed into the ground, but otherwise there is no reason not to use all the ornamental lighting techniques possible for other areas. The illumination may be a little more low-key than in rear-garden areas, and some homeowners may prefer to have it cabled to a separate switch from driveway or house wall lights, so it can be used more selectively.

### Preserving a vista

If the balanced view we have achieved between distant focal point, background, and middle ground is to be appreciated, the foreground lighting must be subtle and subdued if we are to see beyond it to the more distant panorama. Leaving the foreground unlit

below: Switching on the garden lighting after a snowfall can create a seasonal surprise.

can distort the perspective, however, because the outer view will appear closer than it really is. Gentle, low-level lighting of foreground features, such as urns, architectural planting, or the low branches of a tree near the patio, will frame the view and maintain perspective. This is particularly important where the distant view is just that—distant.

One situation in which garden lighting, whether ornamental or practical, will be secondary to anything else is the balcony, roof garden or hillside terrace with a city view or perhaps a seascape. In these locations, the view outward will have priority and any artificial lighting within the area will have only a supporting role. The task here is to preserve the view, which may be achieved by framing it through subtle lighting of plants or structures, or by introducing lighting within the space to cater for eating and entertaining but that can be controlled at will, with separate switches for different lighting functions and moods. The same applies in larger gardens where you wish to see the illuminated garden rather than any brightly lit areas near the house or viewpoint. Switching off area lighting close to you will enable you to see the view beyond the patio.

### Outdoor rooms

These days, gardens are often divided into several "rooms," which are separate from each other, may have different uses, and may or may not be directly visible from the house or patio. If there is a swimming pool, for example, we do not necessarily want to see the area around it when we look out of a window.

When there are several rooms within a single garden, individual vistas may appear differently according to the part of the garden from which they are seen, or a view may be seen unexpectedly as you walk from one part of the garden to another. The lighting scheme might, therefore, have to include separate switches for lighting within each garden room while at the same time taking into account

the layout of the entire garden and the need to provide lighting for access between the different rooms within the garden. There are occasions, however, when multiple viewpoints will not make any difference to the controls: a front garden should be attractively lit whether someone is entering or leaving the house or simply looking at it through a window.

## Creating flexibility

For every type of garden activity, there are a host of personal variations. Just as the design of the garden itself is determined by the style of the house and the personality of the owner, the lighting scheme will be similarly affected. In addition, the lighting must take into account the lifestyle of the homeowner and reflect constraints imposed by the seasons. For example, it may be important to be able to light the garden for both large parties and intimate gatherings. Someone with a large garden might even want a scheme that allows a range of activities to be

carried out in different parts of the garden at the same time. Lighting must also be flexible enough to suit the mood of the occasion. At the end of a meal, being able to direct light toward a table is less important than lighting the view from the patio.

Seasonal changes may necessitate alterations in the way that lighting is used. Some people will want a lighting scheme that allows them to look over the garden from a conservatory or sitting room in winter, or makes barbecues more enjoyable in summer. In winter there is no need to light the herbaceous borders, which will have died down. Moon lighting can look stark when the leaves that provided the dappled shadows have fallen, and underwater lighting will not be needed when the pump has been switched off. Although these may seem obvious points, they are easily overlooked, so that the extra switch or cable needed is omitted from the original plan. Considering all uses of the garden at every time of the year will ensure the

**above:** In winter the dead stems used by flower arrangers can be left, instead of being cut down, to complement evergreen planting and the bare skeletons of deciduous trees. This view from a conservatory is preferable to the black mirror" effect.

# Choosing products

**above:** Lighting effects are all the more intriguing when lights are hidden below decking, behind landscape features, or recessed in the ground. The onlooker's pleasure is heightened by curiosity about how the effects are achieved.

Choosing the fixtures that will meet the needs identified in your plan is the last step in developing a lighting scheme. The models you select should be attractive where possible, but in most cases you will look for those that are unobtrusive: they may be small, colored to blend in with their surroundings, recessed, or they may have all three character-istics. In addition, you will want to select products that are reliable and easy to maintain.

## Weatherproof or waterproof?

The first consideration is that the fixtures must be weatherproof or waterproof enough to perform their required functions. The two terms are not interchangeable. Lights for use underwater must be waterproof in the true sense of the word and keep the bulb and electrical parts dry even when the fixture is submerged in water, otherwise they present a great danger. Most lights, however, will not be used underwater, and it will suffice that they are weatherproof. In most cases, they should be rainproof—that is, proof against water spray from above—while others will have to be suitable for use where hoses and irrigation systems may result in water spray from the side or even from below. This does not always mean that water is totally excluded, merely that any water that enters has no harmful effects. Many wall lights and lanterns, for example, are constructed so that any water trickling in around the edge of glazing panels will run harmlessly out of the fixture without touching any live electrical parts. However, be sure to read the safety labels on the packages carefully before you install any lighting.

## Dust and insects

The other elements that must be guarded against are solid ones. Dust blowing into a fixture will need more frequent cleaning, and nest-building by ants may result in a buildup of material that can cause a circuit breaker to trip out. It is also important to protect small children, who may be tempted to experiment by poking objects into holes in a way that might have fatal results.

## IP ratings

Fixtures are rated according to their resistance to the ingress of both liquids and solids by a code defining their Index of Protection—often known as an "IP rating"—which you will usually find in the product catalog or specification. The letters IP are followed by two digits. The first of

these quantifies protection against contact with live parts or ingress of solid bodies; the second indicates the level of protection against ingress of liquid. The box on page 106 provides a key to these figures and an explanation of their meaning. The figure 4 indicates the minimum standard acceptable for most exterior applications.

Many line-voltage wall lights, column-mounted lanterns, and bollard lights are rated from IP44 and include drainage holes to deal with any moisture that penetrates into the mounting. Some spike- and surface-mounted spotlights, especially those made from aluminum or copper spinnings, have a rating of IP54 or IP55. They rely on some degree of

**below:** Luminaires need to be more than rainproof where pressure washers, hoses, or irrigation systems are in use.

## INDEX OF PROTECTION (IP) RATINGS

| FIRST NUMERAL | | SECOND NUMERAL | |
|---|---|---|---|
| NUMBER/ SYMBOL | DEGREE OF PROTECTION | NUMBER/ SYMBOL | DEGREE OF PROTECTION |
| 4 | (a) Protection against contact by tools, cables, or the like, more than 1 mm thick.<br>(b) Protection against ingress of small foreign bodies. | 4 | Splash proof: liquid splashed from any direction shall have no harmful effect. |
| 5 | (a) Complete protection against contact.<br>(b) Dustproof: protection against harmful deposits of dust; dust may enter but not in amount sufficient to interfere with satisfactory operation. | 5 | Jet proof: water projected by a nozzle from any direction (under stated conditions) shall have no harmful effect. |
| 6 | (a) Complete protection against contact.<br>(b) Dust-tight: protection against ingress of dust. | 6 | Watertight equipment: protection against conditions on ship's decks, etc. Water from heavy seas or power jets shall not enter the enclosures under prescribed conditions. |
| **IP CODE NOTES**<br>• Degree of protection is stated in form IPXX.<br>• Protection against contact or ingress of water respectively is specified by replacing first or second X by digit number tabled, e.g., IP2X defines an enclosure giving protection against finger contact but without any specific protection against ingress of water or liquid.<br>• Example: an underwater light should be rated at IP68.<br><br>**Use this table for general guidance only.** | | 7 | Protection against immersion in water: it shall not be possible for water to enter the enclosure under stated conditions of pressure and time. |
| | | 8 | Protection against indefinite immersion in water under specified pressure: it shall not be possible for water to enter the enclosure. |

drainage because this method of construction makes it difficult to achieve a complete water seal. Spotlights made from aluminum or brass castings are usually machined and gasketed to achieve a rating of at least IP55, while lights to be recessed into walls or the ground need to be rated to at least IP56, so that they are safe from regular splashing or water spray. Underwater lights or recessed lights to be used in ground subject to waterlogging should be rated at IP68.

While these protection ratings are a good guide to a light's suitability for exterior use, they can realistically be achieved only when the equipment is correctly installed and used. Wall-mounted fixtures commonly require seals or sealants around fixing holes and cable entries, and these are usually specified in the instruction leaflets supplied by the manufacturers. Equally, underwater lights cannot be expected

**above:** Recessed brick lights are a neat means of providing low-level area lighting around a patio or along a path.

to retain a waterproof cable entry if they are dragged around a pond during weed clearance or other maintenance.

## Surface or recessed lights?

Recessed uplights are often chosen because burying the fixture in the ground seems the best way to uplight a subject without the light source being visible. Uplighting a tree growing out of a lawn with a flush recessed uplight will allow mowing to be carried out without the risk of damaging the fixture or creating a trip hazard, which would occur with a spike-mounted uplight in the same place. In any open area, be it gravel, decking, or paving, a neatly recessed fixture will always be preferable for unobtrusive lighting. In other positions, however, a spike-mounted spotlight may be more flexible and less expensive, provided it can be hidden among low planting so it does not become a focal point in itself.

The same debate—surface or recessed—often arises with wall lights, especially low-level lighting used for steps. Recessed lights positioned flush in a wall will always be less obtrusive than surface-mounted ones, and often the limited area—a small area of step, path, or patio—means that the extra

bulk of an adjustable fixture is not acceptable. There are times, however, when fitting recessed lighting can be difficult or impossible, because cabling to the fixtures is not easy, but more often because the type of material used in wall construction will not permit it, as with timber constructions. Surface-mounted lights are therefore more commonly used in association with wooden decking.

**above:** This recessed metal halide uplight has an adjustable bulb holder to allow the light beam to be focused in both direction and beam angle. A little condensation on the inside of the lens is common when the air trapped inside is humid and does no harm.

**left:** An adjustable, spike-mounted copper spotlight is a compact and versatile unit to use at the front of a border where planting may not hide it completely.

| SPOTLIGHTS VERSUS UPLIGHTS | | |
|---|---|---|
| | ADVANTAGES | DISADVANTAGES |
| **Spike-mounted spotlights** | • Easily moved and focused | • Obtrusive unless hidden by planting |
| | • Adjustable head gives flexibility | • Easily knocked out of position |
| | • Relatively inexpensive | • Cabling susceptible to damage by dogs |
| **Recessed uplights** | • Unobtrusive in open areas | • Only limited internal adjustment possible |
| | • Can be mowed or swept over | • More expensive than spike-mounted units |
| | • Minimize trip hazard | • Easily covered by fallen leaves and other debris |
| | | • Liable to internal condensation |
| | | • Hot lenses can pose problems in paths and decks |

## Finishes and materials

The best garden lighting will be made from durable materials—aluminum, copper, brass, and stainless steel. Such materials can dissipate heat so that fixtures do not overheat and cause premature bulb failure or distortion of the fixture body. Good heat dissipation means lower lens and body temperatures, which is beneficial when there is accidental contact with the skin. Also, fixture designs can be smaller and less visually obtrusive.

The finish may be a natural one for some metals, which are used in bare or polished form, or an applied color, which is usually a powder coat rather than a liquid paint finish, as a well-applied powder coat is much more durable. Some less expensive products may not have been properly prepared before powder-coating, and the powder coat sometimes peels off after a few years. As with everything, you get what you pay for. Different finishes are best suited to particular applications and locations and these are summarized on page 109.

## Selecting light fittings

For the most commonly used types of garden-lighting products there are a few key points that will make the lighting scheme more aesthetic or durable if the appropriate product choice is made. There are also a few tricks of the trade for various product types and these are mentioned below.

### Spike-mounted uplights and spotlights

Spike-mounted spotlights are the workhorses of most garden-lighting schemes because ground-mounted uplighting is the most common choice for lighting trees, shrubs, columns, and focal points. Spike-mounted fixtures are the usual first choice because they can

| SELECTING FITTINGS FOR THE GARDEN | | |
|---|---|---|
| **MATERIAL** | **COLOR/FINISH** | **USES** |
| **Aluminum** (powder coated) | Green | Spike-mounted spotlights blend with planting. Surface-mounted fittings blend with green-painted and stained timber. |
| | Black | Traditional finish matches architectural hardware, rose arches, and so on. Often inexpensive. |
| | White | Traditional finish matches architectural hardware, window frames, conservatories. |
| | Customized colors | Sometimes available to special order so that fixtures blend or contrast with an existing scheme. |
| | Silver/metal look | Inexpensive alternative to stainless steel for a modern look. |
| **Brass** | Natural | Weathers to blend with light-colored stone, gravel, and pale timber. Polished brass will tarnish unless lacquered. |
| **Bronze** | Natural | Weathers to a darker finish than brass. |
| **Chrome-plated** | Polished | Decorative finish for modern settings. |
| **Copper** | Natural | Weathered, mottled finish blends with timber, brick, gravel, and bark mulch. Eventually weathers to verdigris. Economical and maintenance-free. |
| **Stainless steel** | Polished | Decorative finish for modern settings; durable in coastal locations. |

**above:** These fixtures could be matched to their surroundings: green among planting, black to match other hardware in the area, "granite" in rocks, or "antique copper" near red brick.

**above:** Uplighting through ferns and tree ferns will complement the spread lighting of the steps. Products could be finished in green to blend with the planting or "granite" to match the paving stones.

be adjusted more than recessed fittings and are typically half the price.

Adjustable spotlights should have a bracket or knuckle, which can be locked in position with a screw or nut so they are less likely to be knocked out of focus. A ground spike with fins rather than just a tubular stem will help to prevent the spotlight from rotating in loose soil if the cable to it is disturbed (pegging down the cables leading to spotlights can also help to avoid such disturbances). A fitted glare guard is essential if the flexibility of spike-mounted spotlights is not to be limited to near paths or viewpoints where glare can be a problem. Where a glare guard is not available or where its use would make the spotlight too bulky and visible, an internal "honeycomb" louvre will help to shield the lamp from view. Similar criteria apply to the use of surface-mounted spotlights on walls, pergolas, and trees.

### Recessed uplights

Internal adjustability of the bulb housing is the main requirement if a recessed uplight is to be used to light

one side of the vertical, so check that adjustability is possible—usually up to 15–20 degrees either side of vertical. Where the location is a route for pedestrians or traffic, a grid accessory over the top of the fixture will prevent a foot from coming into contact with a hot lens or a stone stuck in the tread of a car tire from puncturing the glass. Corrosion by ground salts can be a major problem with recessed uplights, particularly if the soil is especially acidic or alkaline. Brass fixtures are largely immune, and many higher-power fixtures are supplied with a plastic sleeve that cradles the metal housing of the fixture and holds it clear of the surrounding soil. It is common to protect aluminum- and steel-bodied fixtures, even when they have been powder-coated or enameled, by painting the recessed parts with a bituminous coating or adding a layer of washed sand around them when they are inserted into the ground. Drainage is also required under recessed lights to make sure they do not become waterlogged. Dig the hole

mounted, as it will make it easy to adjust them and replace the bulbs in future years.

### Spread lights

This type of fixture is highly visible in the garden because it needs to stand to a given height to spread a pool of light around it. Cast-aluminum alternatives are preferable where children are likely to test the strength of the fittings, and these are available in a variety of colors to blend with the background or to match other garden hardware. Copper spread lights are particularly popular for their natural weathered appearance. Look for designs with a glass dome or tube to protect the bulb and its holder from irrigation or hose spray. Some models are available with a choice of ground spike and surface mounting. The latter is especially useful if you want to fix spread lights around decking or the edge of planters, for example.

**left:** A brass underwater light, used without its usual fixing bracket and installed as a small recessed uplight, is hard to see among the pebbles surrounding the phormium.

**below:** A modern style in a traditional material: this small, halogen bollard light weathers to an attractive brown patina, which blends well with brick and gravel and contrasts pleasantly with planting.

at least half as deep again as the fixture's depth and fill the bottom with clean gravel before locating the fixture in the ground. Do not use recessed uplights where regular waterlogging of the ground occurs unless they have an IP68 rating.

### Underwater lights

All underwater lights, which must be rated at IP68 at least, should be equipped with a robust bracket with screw-locking adjustment so the fixture's focus can be maintained even in rough water. The fixture will usually be fixed to an underwater block to anchor it in place, and all fixings must be either stainless steel or brass to be corrosion-proof. Most fixing screws used by manufacturers are stainless steel, and there may be a reaction with the material of the body, which makes the screw stick in place after a time, particularly with aluminum bodies. It's good to smear screw threads with synthetic grease or petroleum jelly. Do this for all garden lights, whether they will be used underwater, recessed, or surface-

# Planning
# the system

above: Lighting trees at the end of the garden means running wires around the garden, preferably during landscaping.

When you have decided on the subjects to light and the lighting effects you want to achieve, try a nighttime demonstration of the new lighting scheme to make sure you are satisfied. The next stage then is to formalize the lighting scheme into a plan. Even an outline plan will help to get wires into the right places during landscaping.

## MAKING A PLAN

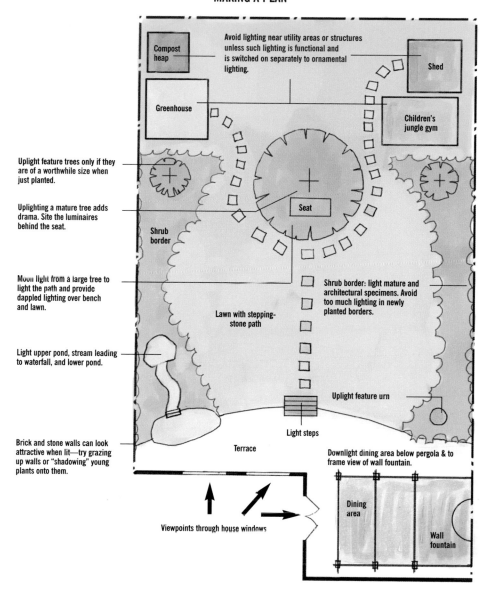

**Compost heap**

Avoid lighting near utility areas or structures unless such lighting is functional and is switched on separately to ornamental lighting.

**Shed**

**Greenhouse**

**Children's jungle gym**

Uplight feature trees only if they are of a worthwhile size when just planted.

Uplighting a mature tree adds drama. Site the luminaires behind the seat.

**Seat**

**Shrub border**

Moon light from a large tree to light the path and provide dappled lighting over bench and lawn.

Shrub border: light mature and architectural specimens. Avoid too much lighting in newly planted borders.

**Lawn with stepping-stone path**

Light upper pond, stream leading to waterfall, and lower pond.

Uplight feature urn

Brick and stone walls can look attractive when lit—try grazing up walls or "shadowing" young plants onto them.

**Light steps**

**Terrace**

Downlight dining area below pergola & to frame view of wall fountain.

**Dining area**

Viewpoints through house windows

**Wall fountain**

If you are going to install a lighting system in an established garden you will need to start by drawing up a scale plan of the garden. Measure the key dimensions and draw the outline of buildings and structures, hard surfaces, such as paths, drives, and patios, key focal points, such as statues or urns, water features, and feature planting, or trees. You will need to include details of boundary walls and fences if you intend to run wires along them or mount transformers and other electrical equipment on them.

Mark on the plan the viewpoints by means of an arrow pointing from the window, seat, door, or gateway to the feature intended to take "center stage" in that particular view.

### USING SYMBOLS

Once you have made a plan, you can start to mark the positions of the luminaires. Use symbols so that you can easily tell when you come back to your diagram what type of luminaire you had planned in each position, what type of wiring you were using, and so on. In small schemes, a simple system of letters to represent different features may suffice, or you could use a system of graphic symbols with a key so that you can tell what each represents.

In larger schemes with a greater variety of items, numbered symbol listings can be used with annotation to indicate information on bulbs and accessories.

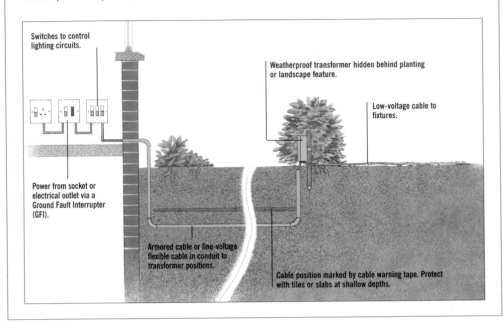

## CABLING AND CIRCUIT PROTECTION FOR A SMALL LOW-VOLTAGE SYSTEM

If the features you wish to light in your garden are near the house and do not need large numbers of high-powered fixtures, then the practical solution is to light your garden using a small low-voltage cable run. All such circuits must be protected by a GFI, and transformers used in the garden must be appropriate for outside use.

Switches to control lighting circuits.

Weatherproof transformer hidden behind planting or landscape feature.

Low-voltage cable to fixtures.

Power from socket or electrical outlet via a Ground Fault Interrupter (GFI).

Armored cable or line-voltage flexible cable in conduit to transformer positions.

Cable position marked by cable warning tape. Protect with tiles or slabs at shallow depths.

## Cabling a low-voltage system

In many gardens the features to be illuminated will not be close to the house, where the power source and switches are located, so the fixtures will be too far away to run on a 12-volt cable from a transformer in the house. This is because of the effect known as "cable voltage drop," which means that the longer the cable is and the more lights that are connected to it (especially if these are higher wattage lights), the more the voltage falls in the cable. If you start with 12 volts from a transformer, there is a limit to how far you can go and to how many lights can be connected to one cable. The practical result of too much voltage drop in the cables from the transformer to a halogen bulb in a garden light is that the bulb will be dimmer than it should be and the light output will be yellow rather than white. A reduction of 10 percent in voltage will reduce the light output of the bulb by a quarter, so a 50-watt bulb run at under 11 volts will achieve little more light output than a fully run 35-watt bulb.

### Low-voltage cable runs

Regulations and local practice vary between countries, so no universal rule can be given for cable length or loading. In the United States, it is usual to have relatively few transformers and long runs, often of thicker cable. Alternatively use a multiple volt transformer that will "transform" voltage from 110 or 220 to 12 volts.

Your lighting or electrical adviser will normally recommend a 12 awg or 14 awg cable. This will maintain light output within 85 percent of the bulb's rated performance and will maintain its color temperature within 5 percent of its rated temperature.

Heavier-gauge cables—ones with thicker, copper cores—can be used to overcome cabling problems where excavating a deep trench for a line-voltage cable has to be avoided, but mixing too many cable sizes in one garden is rarely a good idea. It is best to use the common cable sizes and to locate transformers close enough to the fixtures so that cable voltage drop remains within required limits.

If you use fixtures with lower-wattage bulbs and the number of fixtures required exceeds the number that can be connected to one cable, then dividing the fixtures onto two or more cables should overcome the difficulty. The problem is avoided with many low-voltage plastic lighting kits simply because the power of the bulbs used is so low that it does not lead to significant cable voltage drop.

### Transformers

A transformer is an electrical or electronic device that changes voltage from one level to another. In garden lighting, this is usually from the line-voltage to 12 volts. The circuit will require secondary fusing. Low-voltage cable runs from the transformer to the fixtures. It usually runs under mulch and over garden structures, although it may need to be protected in a conduit, either for practical reasons or to comply with local regulations.

To minimize cable voltage drop to the fixtures, look at the location of the fixtures you have marked on your plan and identify groups of lights that can be supplied from one central transformer. Check that the transformer location is within the length of the low-voltage cable permitted. If the low-voltage cable runs are too long, divide the lights into smaller groups that can be cabled from two or more transformers. In many back gardens, a typical arrangement may require one transformer on each side of the garden and perhaps one transformer to cover features at the far end of the garden. A simple way of checking cable runs on a plan is to use a pair of compasses to measure the radius of a

**CABLING AND CIRCUIT PROTECTION FOR A LARGER GARDEN LIGHTING SYSTEM INVOLVING MULTIPLE CIRCUITS**

Auxiliary fuseboard or distribution board for exterior circuits must include GFI protection.

Separate switches for front and rear garden lighting.

Line voltage cables may be armored or flexible types in a conduit, and are laid below the level where soil may be disturbed to transformers or line-voltage fixtures.

Powerful uplights require line-voltage input.

circle based on the maximum cable run from the proposed site of the transformer.

Transformers for exterior use are housed in weatherproof boxes, which come in many shapes and sizes. They can normally be hidden behind planting and landscape features. For locations where transformers cannot be hidden, special ground-burial types are available, but surface-mounted units are preferable because they are always easier to maintain. These should be installed by a professional.

### Calculating transformer size

People planning a lighting system for the garden often ask how many lights can be run from a single transformer. In fact, transformers are available in a range of wattage ratings, and a more appropriate question would be: "What size of transformer is needed to power the lights in the design?" Deciding on a transformer is simply a matter of multiplying the wattage and numbers of the bulbs used in the fixtures to be connected to the transformer.

In most instances, it is sensible to allow some spare capacity within the transformer rating so that there is scope for increasing some of the bulb wattages as plants grow or for adding a fixture in the future. Allow about 25 percent spare capacity when you select a transformer. Transformers are usually available in 50- or 100-watt steps, so it is merely a question of choosing the next step up from the total wattage you have calculated. Avoid loading the transformer to less than two-thirds of its power rating because this can result in "overvoltage," which reduces bulb life.

### Planning a larger system

A plan for a larger system should include more detail than can easily be recorded on a single drawing or sketch plan. The basic plan should give all the essential information about the locations of fixtures, transformers, the source of power, and the position of controls, in addition to details of the cabling. This can be done using graphic symbols or numbered symbols. These can be cross-referenced to notes that provide further details. The main schedule will list all the lighting effects and the bulbs and fixtures specified. It should also define any separation of lighting onto separate circuits and provide an opportunity for noting special requirements, either for switching or for accessories. A second

| EXAMPLES OF CALCULATING TRANSFORMER RATINGS | | | | | |
|---|---|---|---|---|---|
| TYPE OF FIXTURE | NUMBER OF FIXTURES | BULB WATTAGE | TOTAL WATTAGE | SPARE CAPACITY | TRANSFORMER RATING (WATTS) |
| **Example 1** | | | | | |
| Spike-mounted spotlight | 3 | 50 | 150 | | |
| Wall-mounted spotlight | 2 | 20 | 40 | | |
| Spread light | 2 | 20 | 40 | | |
| Total | 7 | | 230 | + 70 | = 300 |
| **Example 2** | | | | | |
| Recessed uplight | 1 | 75 | 75 | | |
| Underwater light | 1 | 35 | 35 | | |
| Step light | 1 | 20 | 20 | | |
| Tree-mounted downlight | 1 | 20 | 20 | | |
| Total | 4 | | 150 | + 50 | = 200 |

**left:** Examples of garden lighting transformers: from left—transformer in weatherproof, wall-mounting box with cable input and output; transformer sealed into wall-mounting enclosures with cable entries; ground-burial transformer kit with plastic potting kit for on-site sealing.

schedule should list the transformers in relation to the circuit to which they are connected, and detail the lights powered from each.

A larger scheme may include front and rear gardens, a pool area, and a children's play area. The rear garden element may include an ornamental lighting circuit for a water feature, trees, and shrubs, plus separate circuits for path lighting, terrace lighting and wall lights on the house itself. Lighting circuits may be switched on and off separately and from different locations, which may include the sitting room and dining room, as well as weatherproof switches in the pool area. This means that the garden and path lighting can be switched on when leaving the pool area if darkness falls while you are enjoying an evening by the pool. The pool and play area lighting may also be switched on and off at different places.

**below:** The ambience of this garden scene is created by using different lighting techniques to accentuate the dining area, pond, and features, such as the urns and architectural plants.

# Implementation
# and installation

Installation of any electrical equipment in gardens is a job for a qualified electrical contractor, especially if water is involved, but understanding some of the issues that need to be considered will help you when drawing up an installation brief for your contractor that reflects your requirements. It may also help the installation to run more smoothly, and the finished scheme will certainly be more successful if you appreciate how the various parts of the project relate to one another.

## Safety

Installing electricity in the garden is not a job for amateurs, and electrical equipment in the garden can be lethal if incorrectly installed or if inadequate provisions have been made in the event of an equipment fault. Water is the main threat. It can seep in through joints and gaskets; be drawn into electrical enclosures by capillary action; form by repeated condensation cycles, and penetrate aging materials which corrode, crack, or are damaged by wildlife, pets, children, careless gardening, or just time. Water conducts electricity and since the ground is usually damp to some extent or other in most countries, the contact of human feet with the ground is all that is needed to provide a fatal route for electrical current. Always make sure outdoor cabling is grounded and is rated as water-resistant U.L.-approved for outdoor use. Fixtures rated for interior use should never be used outdoors. Proper circuit protection for all exterior electrical services should include a ground fault interruptor (GFI). This simple device ensures that the power is cut off immediately when it detects a leakage of current to earth, which indicates an electrical fault potentially threatening to life. So, observe a few simple rules and keep your garden safe.

## Who does what?

Bear in mind that although an electrical contractor may be qualified to install the system, few electricians have much experience in designing garden lighting systems. You may already have decided to seek the services of a garden lighting specialist to prepare the lighting design you need and to draw up the plan. You may pay a fee for this service, although some specialists will provide the design service as part of a package that includes sourcing products from manufacturers and installation. Some landscape contractors may be able to provide this service as well as lay the cables in the garden during landscape works. Finding a garden lighting specialist is becoming easier as the market grows and new companies emerge. Searching directories or asking friends and garden designers for recommendations can now be supplemented by searching the Internet under "garden lighting" or "landscape lighting." Whoever you choose to help with design or installation, look for evidence of experience in testimonials, recommendations, and photographs of completed projects.

## Power for the system

Garden lighting is rarely installed as the only equipment that is run by electricity in a garden, and these other services must be taken into account. This does not mean that the power for all equipment must come from the same place. Lighting is slightly different in that convenience usually demands that the switches are in the house or on the patio. Most other services, such as supplies to exterior electrical sockets, sheds, and irrigation controllers, are

| DO | DON'T |
| --- | --- |
| • Employ a qualified electrical contractor for all garden electrical installations.<br>• Ensure that all exterior electrical circuits are protected by a GFI.<br>• Have your system tested by a qualified electrical contractor if you have any doubts.<br>• Turn electrical equipment off before performing any maintenance function, even just changing a bulb. | • Install electrical equipment outside unless you are qualified to do so.<br>• Use switches, sockets, transformers or any other electrical devices in the garden if they are designed for interior installation.<br>• Protect electrical equipment with plastic bags or temporary wrappings as a substitute for proper weatherproof enclosures. |

either unswitched or, like timers to control fountain pumps, which may need to be turned off at night, are switched by other means.

It may not always be possible to provide power from the house because existing hard landscaping would make it difficult and disruptive to lay cables. Sometimes the power for the lighting is taken from a supply in the garage, pool house, greenhouse, or other outside building, and control may be provided by remote controls or automatic devices.

### Power for simple systems

Many systems need only a limited amount of power. A small system with a few spotlights for ornamental effect, an additional path or patio lighting circuit, and a low-power pump for a water feature will consume less than 5 amps of power. These can usually be cabled as a spur from an electrical socket, via a GFI, a small switch panel, and a junction box to connect the exterior cables.

### Power for larger systems

When lighting is provided for a large property, the total exterior electrical load can be both high and complex, including lighting, water pumps, and irrigation systems as well as electrical supplies for pools, outbuildings, and electric gates. The amount of power required usually dictates that the electrical source for exterior circuits should come from the main electrical supply, preferably via a GFI to provide essential safety protection and circuit breakers to provide protection against overloads and short-circuits.

In very large installations, where the house has a three-phase electrical supply, there are a number of different options. The exterior circuits may be taken from one phase; from selected circuits of different phases to balance the load; or, where the total amount of electrical power required is very high, from a separate three-phase supply. The advantage of taking exterior circuits from the incoming supply is that the circuit protection is separate for interior and exterior circuits, so that an exterior fault

in a fixture, pump cable, or garden socket will not make interior circuits trip.

### Laying cables

Providing cables for complex electrical systems in large gardens should be done by an electrical engineer. Although some general guidelines apply to all gardens, these may be affected by local regulations and practices. For example, flexible cable in conduits is quite common in the United States.

The amount of line-voltage cable required for garden lighting will be reduced if a low-voltage system is chosen. Flexible, low-voltage cables can be run from transformers that are hidden behind plants and landscape features so that all that is needed is a relatively simple infrastructure of line-voltage cabling to the transformers. Always use type UF cable for installations requiring underground cabling. The UF implies that there must be a fuse or breaker inside the house at the starting point of the underground cabling installation. Line-voltage cables must be buried 18–24 inches below the surface. Using a simple line-voltage cable layout will reduce the amount of digging required. This can be an important factor in an established garden, and digging a trench around the edge of a lawn is generally easier than through mature, well-grown borders.

Apart from the safety considerations of inappropriate cabling, which your contractor will help you to avoid, many misconceptions about electrical cabling based on a limited understanding of household appliances, are transferred to the garden. The most usual mistakes are to have line-voltage cables that are too small for the load or that do not cater to a sufficient number of circuits.

### Cable size

The most common misconception is that the gauge of cabling used for the interior lighting circuit or for the table lamps in the living room is adequate outside. Unfortunately, this ignores the fact that cable voltage drop is often a more important factor in cable selection than the amount of electrical current it has to carry. Indoor cable runs are relatively short, but the amount of lighting in a garden can exceed that on a lighting circuit in the house. For example, 16 awg cable is the minimum size for lighting a small garden, but expecting such a cable to carry power to light large trees 110 yards from the house is unrealistic. The line-voltage cable size must be calculated according to the length of the cable run, so if your garden is anything other than a small one, upgrade to the next cable size, 12 awg or 14 awg.

### Too few cables

The other common mistake is thinking in terms of a single electrical supply into the garden when you actually need several electrical services. One three-core, line-voltage cable may be fine for running the fountain pump during the day and the evening before you switch it off at night, but if you wish to operate the lighting and the pump separately, you will need to have one three-core cable for each function. This also applies to other services, such as power to the shed or the swimming pool. In addition, if you wish to switch on lighting selectively on separate circuits, you will need to lay enough cables to do so. This can either be separate three-core cables to each transformer location on each circuit or a multicore cable to cater to enough circuits. The only other approach is to convert a single electricity supply into multiple functions by using remote or automatic controls, but this is often less convenient and more expensive to install than the familiar wall switch.

### Installing cable in new gardens

Because low-voltage systems require a comparatively simple line-voltage cable layout, they are usually easier to

## LAYING CABLES

Laying electrical cables in the ground may be subject to specific regulations in different countries. The aim is to ensure that the cables are buried deeply enough in the ground (at least 18-24 inches) to avoid any disturbance likely to occur. Where armored cables can be buried at adequate depth, they can be laid in a buffer layer of sand and covered with cable warning tape. Where it is not possible to bury the cables deeply enough because of the presence of tree roots or unsuitable ground conditions, extra mechanical protection around the cables will be required. This is usually in the form of plastic ducts or conduits through which the cables are run. For extra protection, the cable or duct could also be covered with a layer of tiles.

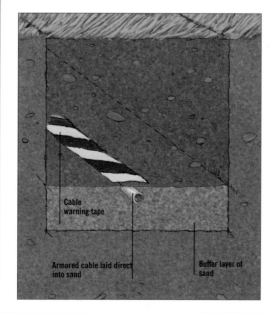

Cable warning tape

Armored cable laid direct into sand

Buffer layer of sand

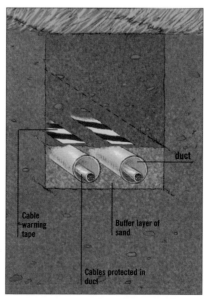

duct

Cable warning tape

Buffer layer of sand

Cables protected in duct

introduce into gardens that are to be newly landscaped. It is often difficult to imagine how the garden will look from a two-dimensional plan, and if your garden is being landscaped professionally, you might find it easier to leave the final design of the lighting scheme until the garden is complete, but to lay cables while the other work is being carried out.

Some cabling must be specific—for example, for uplighting large trees and for any lighting that needs to be built into walls or paving as part of the construction process—but the remainder of the system can be finalized later as long as the line-voltage cable infrastructure has been installed during landscaping. If this is done, it is necessary to prepare only an outline lighting design to establish the transformer positions, numbers of circuits, power source, and switching requirements. The result is a cable plan, which can be implemented by landscapers during the construction work. The lighting scheme can be finalized later.

## Controlling the system

As well as providing enough cables to provide the power needed in the garden, you should also consider the type of switches that you need and the most appropriate places to install them.

### Manual switching

For most systems, a simple switch on the wall is all that is needed. We can use it to switch lights and equipment on and off when we feel like it and have selected lighting on separate switches if we have planned it that way. In most gardens that probably means having one switch for the ornamental garden lighting circuit, one for the downlighting over the pergola or patio, and one for the wall lights on the rear of the house. Extra switches allow us to switch security floodlights on manually for reassurance when we hear a noise outside, and off again so they do not interfere with more subtle lighting. Switches are best sited near to the windows from which the view is seen or the doors through which the garden is entered—the conservatory, lounge, or dining room for the back-garden lighting

| TYPICAL CONTROLS FOR VARIOUS TYPES OF LIGHTING CIRCUIT | |
|---|---|
| **TYPES OF LIGHT** | **TYPES OF CONTROL** |
| Security lighting | Operated by passive infrared movement detectors; override enables lighting to be switched on or off manually; separate control panel for a multi-zone system, possibly linked to alarm system |
| Driveway lighting | Photocell for dawn to dusk operation; timer/photocell or solar dial timer for automatic operation without seasonal adjustment; an alternative to security lighting with movement detectors |
| Entrance lighting | Manually switched or automatic operation as for driveway lighting |
| Facade lighting | Manually switched or automatic operation as for driveway lighting |
| Ornamental lighting | Manually switched by wall-mounted switches or remote controls |
| Path lighting | Manually switched in rear gardens; automatic operation as for driveway lighting in front gardens; two-way switching may be required in larger gardens for paths linking pool areas and so on |
| Patio/terrace lighting | Manually switched; dimmers for enhanced control of ambient lighting in intimate settings |
| Task lighting | Weatherproof switch for barbecue lighting; local switches for tennis court lighting, etc. |
| Gazebo lighting | Local switch inside gazebo for internal downlighting; exterior lighting on ornamental circuit |
| Pool lighting | Manual switching on same panel as poolside and pool-house lighting |

and the entrance hall for the front garden.

Using contractors makes it possible to control the lighting system from several locations or for different types of controls to be used together—for example, linking driveway lighting to security lighting circuits after an automatic timed period and providing manual override facilities.

### Dimmers

The use of dimmers has increased dramatically in recent years and in large gardens they can take the form of sophisticated, "scene-setting" systems in which a computerized controller will set several lighting circuits to create functional or mood-related lighting setups in reception rooms. Dimmers are not generally recommended for garden lighting, for several reasons. If both the garden and the garden lighting system have been well-designed, the lighting should not need significant adjustment to its brightness to provide interest all year round. Adjustments to brightness can be made by changing bulb beams and wattages to achieve the correct balance in the design. Some types of garden lighting—metal halide lighting for large trees and compact fluorescent bulbs in wall lights, for example—are not suitable for use with dimmers and can be damaged by them. Special types of dimmers must be used with low-voltage lighting. In addition, simple wall dimmers are limited in power rating to under 400 watts, which is less than the power of a typical garden lighting circuit, except in a very small garden.

Small, intimate spaces where the lighting level can dramatically affect the ambience of the occasion are an exception—courtyard, balcony, and roof gardens, and alfresco dining areas are examples, especially where dimming the lighting can enable you to see a vista beyond.

### Remote controls

If power has to be taken from a location where switches would be inconvenient, fitting a remote control unit is one way of making the system easier to use.

Radio remote controls are now available in FM long-range versions that are capable of switching on lighting up to 325 yards away. This is a theoretical "line of sight" range, which is reduced by the presence of large trees, metal structures, and buildings.

### Photocells and timers

Photocells are electronic devices that sense ambient daylight levels and switch on lighting when it gets dark and switches it off again at dawn. This is a simple method of automatic control if you want lighting on all night. Check that photocells are suitable for use with compact fluorescent bulbs if you wish to use these for their long bulb life.

You can use a photocell in conjunction with a timer so that the photocell switches the lighting on when dusk falls, and the timer switches the lighting off at a chosen time. This is a popular method of control where all-night lighting is not required. Timers usually have the facility for manual override and are available in both 24-hour and 7-day versions. Special types, which automatically adjust for seasonal changes, are available.

### Movement detectors

Movement detectors are normally associated with security lighting. They can be used with low-voltage transformers and are well suited to driveways. Passive infrared detectors monitor heat sources—usually body heat or heat from vehicles. Beam detectors of the type commonly used with electric gates may also be used to switch on the lighting. This method of control provides convenient automatic switching without expensive or disruptive cabling. Lighting the way from a garage to the side door of the house so that the light switches on when you step into range and off again after a timed period is a good example.

# Glossary

**Absorption:** The amount of light taken in by a surface instead of being reflected.

**Accent Lighting:** The highlighting of individual features.

**Adaptation:** The process which takes place as the eye adjusts to variations in brightness within its field of vision.

**Ambient Lighting:** Soft, indirect illumination.

**Beam Angle:** The angle of coverage of the pattern of light produced by a reflector lamp or by the combination of a bulb and a reflector.

**Black Mirror Effect:** The effect which makes window glass a dark reflective mirror at night.

**Cable Voltage Drop:** A reduction in electrical pressure in a cable resulting from increasing distance from the power source or increased power (wattage or current) drawn along the cable. Higher wattage lamps positioned further away from a transformer will experience reduced voltage, which reduces light output and can inhibit efficient operation of the halogen cycle.

**Color Rendering:** A comparative term to describe how well a lamp illuminates an object's colors compared with daylight.

**Contrast:** The difference in appearance of two parts of a visual field seen simultaneously or successively.

**Diffused Lighting:** Illumination which appears to come from many directions, or at least is not dependent on a light beam from one direction.

**Diffusion Filter:** A frosted or opal glass lens that is used to widen or soften light output.

**Dimming:** The control of the light output from the light source by electrical or resistive methods.

**Directional Lighting:** Lighting designed to illuminate an object or surface predominantly from a chosen direction.

**Direct Lighting:** Lighting in which the greater part of the illumination reaches a surface directly, i.e., without reflection from other surfaces.

**Disability Glare:** Glare which impairs the ability to see detail.

**Discharge lamp:** A lamp in which bright, energy-efficient light is produced by electrically-exciting, pressurized gas in a bulb.

**Discomfort Glare:** Glare which causes visual discomfort.

**Fiber-Optic Lighting:** A system of projecting light along a bundle of optical glass fibers.

**Filter:** A glass or metal accessory which alters the characteristics (shape, color, etc.) of light beam patterns.

**Fluorescent lamp:** A lamp in which energy-efficient light is produced by electrically exciting a phosphor coating on the inside surface of a glass tube or container.

**Glare:** The discomfort or impairment of vision experienced when parts of the visual field are excessively bright in relation to the general surroundings.

**Illuminance:** The concept of illumination falling on to a surface. The unit of measurement in the U.S. is the foot candle.

**Illumination:** The process of lighting an object or surface.

**Indirect Lighting:** Lighting in which the greater part of the illumination reaches a surface only after reflection from other surfaces.

**Incandescent lamp:** A bulb in which light is produced by a filament (usually made of halogen) heated to incandescence by the passage of an electric current through it.

**Kelvin:** Degrees Kelvin (K) is a measure of the color temperature of light.

**Lightbulb:** Layman's term for a lamp, i.e., a glass container with a coating, filament, or gas which glows when electricity is applied.

**Line Voltage:** Household electricity supply. The standard in North America is 120 volts.

**Louvre:** An open grid of translucent or opaque elements attached to a fixture in such a position that the bulbs cannot be seen directly above a given angle, normally the maximum beam angle of the bulbs fitted.

**Luminaire:** An apparatus which includes all the components necessary for fixing and protecting lamps and for connecting them to the supply circuit. Also called a "fixture."

**Mercury Vapor Lamp:** High intensity discharge lamp in which light is emitted mainly as a result of electrical excitation of mercury compounds within a bulb.

**Metal Halide Lamp:** High-intensity discharge lamp in which light is emitted as a result of electrical excitation of metal halides within a bulb.

**Mirror Reflector Lamp:** A type of reflector lamp with a mirror-finish reflector to control and direct the light output. Size is denoted in eighths of an inch in diameter; e.g., an MR16 lamp is 2 inches in diameter.

**PAR lamp:** Reflector lamp with a parabolic aluminized reflector. Size is denoted in eighths of an inch in diameter, so, for example, a PAR38 lamp is 4.75 inches in diameter.

**Reflectance:** The ratio of the amount of light reflected from a surface to the illuminance falling upon it.

**Reflector:** A device for controlling the light emitted from a bulb by reflection at suitably shaped surfaces, normally conical or bowl-shaped for spotlights.

**Reflector Bulb:** An incandescent or discharge bulb in which part of the bulb, suitably shaped, is coated internally with a reflecting material which partly controls the distribution of light emitted from the bulb.

**Spread Lens:** A glass lens used to diffuse and widen or elongate light beam patterns.

**Transformer:** A magnetic or electronic device which increases or decreases voltage; mainly used for low voltage lighting.

**Voltage:** A measurement of electrical pressure through a cable or electrical apparatus.

**Wattage:** The power rating, measured in watts, of a lamp or electrical apparatus.

# Index

# Acknowledgments

In Source Order

**Emap Gardening Picture Library** 23 top, 24 bottom, 39 top.

**Elizabeth Whiting Associates**/Tim Street Porter 49 bottom.

**Andrea Jones/Garden Exposures**/Trevyn McDowell's roof garden, Clerkenwell, courtesy Channel 4 series *Garden Doctors* 4–5, 52 top.

**Garden Picture Library**/Andrew Payne 91, /Gary Rogers 117 bottom, /Ron Sutherland/ Eco Design, Melbourne 66 bottom.

**Jerry Harpur**/Design: Grover Dear, Hong Kong 1, 38, /Design: Topher Delaney, San Francisco 43, 50 top, /Design: Sonny Garcia, San Francisco 6, 97, 101, /Design: Luciano Giubbilei, London 9, 34, 41 top, /Mr. & Mrs. Lerner, California 2, 37, /Longwood, Pennsylvania 55 top, /Design: Made Wijaya, Bali, Indonesia 27 bottom, /Design: Camille Muller, Paris 102, /David Pearson, London 39 bottom, 77, /Design: Dan Pearson, London 118, /Hank Lith and Rod Taylor, South Africa 48t.

**Marcus Harpur**/Princes Trust RHS Chelsea 2000 25 bottom.

**The Interior Archive**/Ed Reeve/Architect: Adajaye & Russell 27 top.

**Lighting for Gardens**/ www.lightingforgardens.co.uk 50 bottom, 51 top, 64, 105, 107 top, 107 bottom, 108, 109, 110, 111 top, 111 bottom, 117 top.

**Marianne Majerus**/Design: Jill Billington 45 top, /Design: George Carter, The Christie Sculpture Garden, RHS Chelsea 1999 46 top, /Design: John Sarbutt 32, /Hotel Tresanton, St Mawes, Cornwall 15, 20, 40, /Design: Mathew Vincent 12, 104, /Design: Stephen Woodhams 7 top, 90 bottom.

**Megabay Lighting Enterprises**/ www.megabay.com (4 Development Court, Caloundra, Queensland, 4551, Australia) 30, 62, 67, 88, 92, 99.

**Clive Nichols Photography**/Garden & Security Lighting 35 top, 56, 112, /Trevyn McDowell & Paul Thompson 90 top, 96, /Design: Natural & Oriental Water Gardens/ Garden & Security Lighting 11, 21, 55 bottom, 63, 83, /The Nichols Gdn, Reading/ Garden & Security

Lighting 57 top, /Peter Reid. 45 bottom, /spidergarden.com/Chelsea 2000 54, /Stephen Woodhams 31.

**Louis Poulsen/Tony Craddock**/ tcr-uk@lpmail.com (Surrey Business Park, Weston Road, Epsom, Surrey, KT17 1JG, UK) 13, 24–25, 48 bottom, 49 top, 65, 69, 93, 94, 95.

**John Raine** 7 bottom, 8 top, 8 bottom, 10 top right, 10 bottom left, 14, 16, 17, 19, 23 bottom, 26, 28, 29, 33, 35 bottom, 36, 41 bottom, 42 top, 42 bottom, 44 top, 44 bottom right, 46 bottom, 47, 51 bottom, 52 bottom, 57 bottom, 61 top, 61 bottom, 66 top, 68 left, 68 right, 73, 74 top, 74 bottom, 75 left, 75 right, 76, 78 top, 78 bottom, 79, 82 top, 82 bottom, 84 top, 84 bottom, 85, 86, 87, 89 top, 89 bottom, 98, 100, 103.

Project Editor: Sarah Ford

Editors: Lydia Darbyshire, Meg Sanders, Cathy Lowne

US Lighting Consultant: Tom Fenig, Outdoor Lighting Perspectives, Charlotte, USAIndex: Indexing Specialists

Executive Art Editor: Geoff Fennell

Designer: Emily Wilkinson

Production Controller: Lucy Woodhead

Picture Research: Zoë Holtermann